What Color Is Your Parachute?

Other Books by Richard N. Bolles

The Three Boxes of Life,
   And How To Get Out of Them

Where Do I Go From Here With My Life?
   (co-authored with John C. Crystal)

*This is an annual. That is to say,
it is substantially revised each year, the
new edition appearing each November.
Those wishing to submit additions,
corrections, or suggestions for the
1998 edition should submit them prior
to February 1, 1997, using the form
provided in the back of this book.
(Forms reaching us after that date will,
unfortunately, have to wait for the
1999 edition.)*

1997 Edition

What Color Is Your Parachute?

A Practical Manual
for
Job-Hunters
& Career-Changers

by

Richard Nelson Bolles

Ten Speed Press

The drawings on pages 104, 116–117, 119, 148–149, and *78–79* are by Steven M. Johnson, author of *What The World Needs Now*.

Library of Congress Catalog Card No. 84-649334
ISBN 0-89815-844-3, paper
ISBN 0-89815-882-6, cloth

Published by Ten Speed Press, P.O. Box 7123, Berkeley, California 94707

Typesetting, Star Type, Berkeley
Printing, Consolidated Printers, Inc.

Contents

Parachute Workbook and Resource Guide

This is dedicated to the one I love
(my wife, Carol)

Preface to the 1997 Edition

This is the 24th annual edition of this book.

The book has grown, not only in number of editions, but also in size. The first edition, self-published in 1970, was 168 pages long. It reached 200 pages with the 1972 edition (when Ten Speed took it over). It reached 300 pages with the 1979 edition. It reached 400 pages with the 1989 edition. And, last year, it reached 480 pages. You can see where all this is heading. (Parenthetically, the reason the book has kept increasing in size, is that the job-market and the job-hunt have gotten so much more complex, over the years -- and there are many more problems to be addressed, if the book is to be truly helpful to all job-hunters and career-changers.)

Over five million people have used this book, and twenty-five thousand people a month go into a bookstore to buy it, these days, despite its middle-age spread. Nonetheless, I have longed for that old *Parachute* -- slim, slender, and easy to get through. I liked that size.

So, with this edition that you hold in your hands, the book has at last divided, like the waters of the Red Sea. Within the same binding, now, are two separate books, with separate covers and separate Tables of Contents: *What Color Is Your Parachute?*, back to the size it was in days of old, containing the information needed by all; and the optional *Parachute Workbook and Resource Guide,* containing the information needed only by some.

The question, of course, is what should be included in the main book -- the section for all? Well, what we have learned over twenty-five years is that job-hunters in general, and the readers of this book in particular, divide into two main groups:

> *Those who want to find employment as quickly as possible,*
> *even if the job isn't an exact match with their dreams.*

and

> *Those who have the time, patience (and money)*
> *to go about the job-hunt more thoroughly,*
> *in order to get the career or job of their dreams.*

Fast vs. *Thorough* are the themes, essentially. Hence, the two subjects covered in the main book, beginning with this edition are: "Tips for the Impatient Job-Hunter," and "Strategies for the Determined Job-Hunter or Career-Changer."

Given the reduced size of this main book, the question then arises: what should be these tips or strategies? My personal approach remains what it has always been: that there are successful vs. unsuccessful job-hunters out there. If we would be successful in our own job-hunt, we must study those job-hunters and career-changers who were successful in their job-hunt, to see what they did. And then copy, adapt, improve, apply what they did, to our own situation.

That is what this book is all about. For twenty-five years now I have been studying, talking to, interviewing individual successful job-hunters, on your behalf, to find out what they did. This book is my annually-updated report of what I found out.

I have also audited and sat in on successful group job-search programs for the unemployed, throughout these twenty-five years. While such programs were actually begun after World War I -- by such names as John Scott (1921), Carl Boll (1933), Sidney Eklund (1935), Alphonso William Rahn (1936), and Bernard Haldane (1946) -- modern group job-search was born *(or reborn)* in the 1970s.

As *Parachute* began during that decade, I interviewed the founders of all of those successful programs. The programs were these:

The Job-Club (1972), conceived by Nathan Azrin at Carbondale, Illinois, and later tested successfully as a WIN (Work Incentive) model in 1978.

Self-Directed-Placement (1974), conceived by Chuck Hoffman, in San Diego.

The Job Factory (1976), conceived by Joseph Fischer and Albert Cullen, in Cambridge, Massachusetts.

The Perschau WIN MODEL (1980), conceived by the late Dave Perschau, in Sonoma County, California, and based on Chuck Hoffman's group job-search methods, plus the WIN (Work Incentive) model of the Department of Labor.

These programs all had two characteristics: a high rate of placement, and in a remarkably short time.

In preparation for writing tips for "The Impatient Job-Hunter" this year, I thought it was time for me to go revisit the ideas of the earliest pioneers, ranging from John Scott to Bernard Haldane (talked to him). I also thought it was time to study once again all those programs of the '70s (easily done, since I have all their manuals). In the course of this study in January and February of 1996, I talked at length with some of those pioneers of the '70s (most notably and helpfully, Nathan Azrin and Chuck Hoffman), plus the modern-day heir to Dave Perschau's program/the WIN model, Dean Curtis of Curtis and Associates in Kearney, Nebraska. I audited his training program, talked with him at length on more than one occasion, and attended his conference on welfare reform in May, 1996.

Furthermore, I resurrected the fine critiques of group job-search programs done by Miriam Johnson and the late Bob Wegmann -- the two best researchers the field of job-search has ever had.

I met briefly with Miriam this year, and spent much time re-reading Bob's fine research, done often with Miriam's assistance: "Job-Search Assistance: A Review," (in the *Journal of Employment Counseling,* vol. 16, #4, December 1979); "Job-Search Assistance During Periods of High Unemployment," an unpublished article (1979); "Job-Search Assistance Programs: Implications for the School," (in the *Phi Delta Kappan,* December 1979); and "Reemployment Assistance for Laid Off Workers," another unpublished article (1983).

Now, I mention all of this research and all of these people, because you will find their fingerprints (as it were) on many of the pages of "The Impatient Job-Hunter." It would weary you, if I were to stop and acknowledge whose idea is whose, each time one is mentioned, so I thought I'd do it here, with my blanket acknowledgement to them all. I thank all those I mentioned above, one and all, for every helpful idea their inventive minds conceived, to help today's job-hunters.

Acknowledging each idea is, in fact, a herculean task, for it is often difficult to know who to attribute an idea to. These group job-search programs of the '70s (and now the '90s) had several characteristics in common: they would (and do) work with *anyone*, including discharged mental patients, prisoners on parole, blue-collar workers, people with serious disabilities, etc.; they all had (or have) startling success rates -- between 66% and 92% of their group members found jobs; *and* this was accomplished within a startlingly short period, running between two to five weeks, typically.

All these programs depended on keeping the group together not only through an instruction period but during the actual job-search and interview process, *all* taught that job-hunting was itself a full-time job, *all* taught self-placement rather than having someone else find the job for you, and *all* depended on heavy use of the telephone to contact employers whether they were known to have a vacancy or not (each job-hunter making as many as 100 phone calls to employers each morning, and 100 phone calls each afternoon).

I have not necessarily used these ideas in the form in which they were adopted in the '70s; rather, for this 1997 edition I have tried to adapt and combine ideas, sometimes stating them in a new way.

And now, in closing, my annual bunch of heartfelt thank yous:

• My thanks first of all to all my readers, and most especially to the two thousand or so, who write me each year. I deeply regret I can no longer answer each individual correspondent. I think authors should answer their mail, and I did so for twenty-five years, sometimes staying up late at night to do so, answering every single letter I ever received; but now at the age of 69, I can no longer keep this up. I landed in the hospital a year or so ago, with a major operation, and I took this to be nature's way of saying, *Slow down.*

Plus, I don't have the stamina I had when I was younger. More importantly, I have a wonderful marriage, and having been a workaholic for twenty-five years or more, I now want to devote more time to enjoying my family. I trust you will understand, and forgive.

I still *read* every one of the letters that come in, and feel that no author could possibly ask for more loving, and appreciative readers -- not in a million years. So if you write me, you can be assured that I will read what you have to say, and ponder it well. But if you need answers -- to requests, invitations, job-hunting problems or questions, I strongly recommend that rather than writing to me you contact instead one of the people near you, who are listed on pp. *249 ff* in *The Parachute Workbook and Resource Guide*.

• My thanks to those creative souls, who first pointed out to me what was wrong with this country's whole job-hunting and career-changing *system*, and gave me documentary evidence of the same -- I think in particular of my friends Dick Lathrop, Sidney Fine, the late Bob Wegmann, Daniel Porot, Tom and Ellie Jackson, Howard Figler, Arthur Miller, Bernard Haldane, Nathan Azrin, Carol Christen, John Holland, Peter Drucker, and -- above all -- the late John Crystal, who gave me the framework of *What, Where and How*. God bless you, John, in your heavenly rest.

• My thanks to my beloved publisher, Phil Wood, who has been a friend as well for over twenty-four years now. My thanks to all the folks over at Ten Speed Press who help get this book out, each year: George Young, my constant help since 1978, Jackie Wan, my proofreader for many years now, the folks at Fifth Street Design who design the cover each year, Bev Anderson, my wonderful lay-out artist for the past twenty-four years, and Linda Davis, our new, caring, typesetter.

• My thanks to my family -- my dear wife, Carol, for her wit, wisdom, and wonderful love over many years; my four grown children, Stephen, Mark, Gary, and Sharon, and my dear step-daughter, Serena; my wonderful sister, Ann Johnson, and last but hardly least, my ninety-three-year-old aunt, Sister Esther Mary, of the Community of the Transfiguration (Episcopal) in Glendale, Ohio, who has taught me to serve the Lord, from my youth up.

Indeed, no litany of thanks would be complete without my thanking The Great Lord God, Father of our Lord Jesus Christ, and source of all grace, wisdom, and compassion, Who has given me this work of helping so many people of different tongues and nations and faiths, with their job-hunt. I am grateful beyond measure for such a life, such a mission, and such a privilege.

Dick Bolles
P. O. Box 379
Walnut Creek
California 94597-0379
7/29/96

My Annual Grammar & Language Footnote

I want to explain three points of grammar, in this book: pronouns, commas, and italics. My unorthodox use of them invariably offends unemployed English teachers so much that they write me to apply for a job as my editor.

To save us unnecessary correspondence, let me explain. Throughout this book, I often use the apparently plural pronoun "they," "them," or "their" after *singular* antecedents --such as, "You must approach *someone* for a job and tell *them* what you can do." This sounds strange and even *wrong* to those who know English well. To be sure, we all know there is another pronoun -- "you" -- that may be either singular or plural, but few of us realize that the pronouns "they," "them," or "their" were also once treated as both plural and singular in the English language. This changed, at a time in English history when agreement in *number* became more important than agreement as to sexual *gender*. Today, however, our priorities have shifted once again. Now, the distinguishing of sexual *gender* is considered by many to be more important than agreement in *number*.

The common artifices used for this new priority, such as "s/he," or "he and she," are -- to my mind -- tortured and inelegant. Casey Miller and Kate Swift, in their classic, *The Handbook of Nonsexist Writing*, agree, and argue that it is time to bring back the earlier usage of "they," "them," and "their" as both singular and plural -- just as "you" is/are. They further argue that this return to the earlier historical usage has already become quite common *out on the street* -- witness a typical sign by the ocean which reads "*Anyone* using this beach after 5 p.m. does so at *their* own risk." I have followed Casey and Kate's wise recommendations in all of this.

As for my commas, they are deliberately used according to my own rules -- rather than according to the rules of historic grammar (which I did learn -- I hastily add, to reassure my old Harvard professors, who despaired of me during English class, weekly). In spite of those rules, I follow my own, which are: I write conversationally, and put in a comma wherever I would normally stop for a breath, were I speaking the same line.

The same conversational rule applies to my use of *italics*. I use *italics* wherever, were I speaking the sentence, I would put *emphasis* on that word or phrase. I also use italics where there is a digression of thought, and I want to maintain the main thought and flow of the sentence. All in all, I write as I speak.

P. S. Over the last twenty-five years, a few critics (very few) have claimed that *Parachute* is too complicated in its vocabulary and grammar for anyone except a college graduate. An Englishman wrote me this year with a different view. He said there is an index that analyzes a book to tell you what grade in school you must have finished, in order to understand it. My book's index, he said, turned out to be 6.1, which means you need only have finished sixth grade in a U.S. school in order to understand it.

Here in the U.S., a college instructor came up with a similar finding. He phoned me to tell me that my book was rejected by the authorities as a proposed text for his college course, because the book's language/grammar was not up to college level. "What level was it?" I asked. "Well," he replied, "when they analyzed it, it turned out to be written on an eighth-grade level."

Sixth or eighth -- that seems just about right to me. Why make things complicated, when they can be expressed simply?

R. N. B.

Well, yes, you do have
great big teeth; but, never mind
that. You were great to at least
grant me this interview.

Little Red Riding Hood

CHAPTER ONE

A Job-Hunting
We Will Go

Okay, this is it.
The moment of truth has arrived
For You. It's time
To go out, and look for a job,
Out there in *the job-market*,
Which all your friends speak of
In hushed tones, as though it were
A battlefield, littered with the bodies
Of the unemployed,
Who tried and failed to find a job
Before you.

You've heard of course
Their stories:
Of graduates
With shiny MBA degrees
Who cannot find
The simplest kind of work.
Of friends who
Studied all the occupational trends,
And then went back to school
To learn the *hot* trade of the moment, but
Can find no work in that *hot* trade,
And two years later are still
Unemployed, angry, or depressed
Beyond all measure.
You've heard
Of people who worked for thirty-five years
For just one place,
And then got downsized
And now are only able
To find temporary work.
You've heard
Of former college profs with two degrees
Working now at the local deli;
Of union workers who went out on strike
Only to find, this time,
Their jobs were not waiting for them, when
They wanted to return,

And now they wander, lost,
   And bewildered,
      For no one told them that if they strike
      They might strike out
       In this *new world.*
        Such sad and tragic stories
        As these
         Are in the papers, everyday;
        And so, we know,
         How well we know,
         What lies in store
         For us, out there
         On the job-market battlefield
         Littered with bodies --
         Eight million of them
         By last count.

        So, now it is our turn,
        And what is it we do,
         When our job-hunting time has come?
       We procrastinate,
      That's what we do.
      We're *busy winding things up,* we say.
      Or, just waiting until we feel a little less
     'Burnt-out,' and more 'up' for the task
    Ahead, we say; though actually,
   If the truth were known,
   We're hoping for *a miracle,*
  You know the one I mean:
 A rescuer, suddenly appearing
On a white horse,
Coming, coming to save us
We don't know
His name: is it
Our former employer,
Or the government,
 Our union,
 Our relatives or friends?
 We are unclear; we only know

The world owes us
  A job.
    It shouldn't be up to us
      To have to go hunting for it,
        So hard, ourselves,
          Although of course we know
          It is precisely up to
          Us.

          So, we make up a glorious resume
          By ourselves or with some help.
          How it sparkles, how it shines,
          How quickly it will get us
          A job.
          We send it out
          By the hundreds,
          By the bushels,
        And then we sit by the phone
        Waiting for that inevitable
       Call,
      From some bright-eyed employer-type
     Who, seeing our glorious history,
    Will cry out *"This is exactly the person*
That we have been looking for!"

  But there is one small problem: the call
   Never comes.
  And we are left to wait
 And wait
 And wait
While the world goes out of its way,
It seems,
To tell us how little
It cares
 Whether we find work,
  Or not.

  We seek out family and friends' advice,
    And the first thing

That they say to us, is,
"Have you tried employment agencies?"
"Why, no," we say,
So down we go.
Down, down, down
To the ante-room, and all those hopeful
Haunted faces.
Our first bout, here,
With *The Dreaded Application Form.*
"Previous jobs held.
List in reverse chronological order."
We answer the questions, then we sit
And wait.
The interviewer, at last, calls us in;
She (or he) of the over-cheerful countenance,
Who we know will give us good advice.
"Let's see, Mr. or Ms.,
What kind of a job are you looking for?"
"Well," say we,
"You can see, there, what I've done.
What do you think?"
She studies, again, our application form;
"It seems to me," she says, *"that with your background*
-- It is a bit unusual --
You might do very well in sales."
"Oh sales," say we. *"Yes, sales,"* says she, *"in fact*
I think I could place you almost immediately.
We'll be in touch. Is this your phone?
I'll call you tomorrow night, at home."
We nod, and shake her hand, and that
Is the last time we ever hear
From her.

We're reduced to the want ads,
By our miserable plight,
But we are dumbfounded
Right there, at the sight
Of those little boxes
Describing jobs that are built

As little boxes
For the soul.
We call on the employers,
We tell them, of course, that we're job-hunting now,
"And your ad looked just right for me . . ." O wow!
Look at that face change, are we in the soup!
As we wait for the heave-ho, the ol' Alley-oop!
Overqualified you say?
Two hundred before me
Have been here already,
And you have only five
Vacancies? No,
Of course I understand."

It is the end of paper, for us.
  We know now that our feet
    Must be pressed
      Into service; so
        Out we go,
          Pounding the pavements,
          Knocking on doors,
            Visiting companies,
              Getting rejected
                At place after place,
                Getting discouraged,
                Day after day,
                  Getting depressed --
                  How pathetic, this is,
                  How crushing to
                  Our self-esteem.

                Weeks drag by,
                Months drag by,
                And we are reeling
                From rejection shock,
                And ever we are thinking:
                  The job-hunt seems the loneliest task in the world.
                  Is it this difficult for other job-hunters
                  Or career-changers?

Well, friend, the answer is YES.

Are other people this discouraged,
   And desperate and depressed,
      And frustrated, and so low in self-esteem after
      A spell of job-hunting?

The answer, again -- unhappily -- is

YES.

   YES.

      YES.

But now, it's time to tell you,
There is something you can do
To change all this.

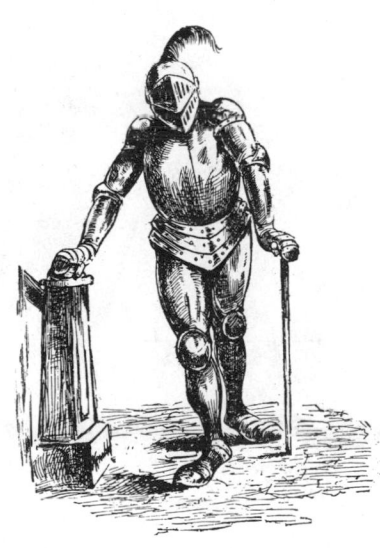

8

It was the best of times,
It was the worst of times,
It was the age of wisdom,
It was the age of foolishness,
It was the epoch of belief,
It was the epoch of incredulity,
It was the season of light,
It was the season of darkness,
It was the spring of hope,
It was the winter of despair,
We had everything before us,
We had nothing before us,
We were all going direct to heaven,
We were all going direct the other way . . .

Charles Dickens
A Tale of Two Cities

CHAPTER TWO

FOR THE IMPATIENT JOB-HUNTER

THERE ARE ALWAYS JOBS OUT THERE

Table of Contents

Chapter 2

Now I know you're patient. *Really*. Normally.

It's just that *time* has become the big issue, for you.

You're out of work, you're running out of money, and the sheriff is closing in. You've *got* to find work -- like: *yesterday*.

You want tips, hints, quick strategies. Briefly described.

You haven't got time for a lot of reading.

You want to get charged up, motivated, filled with hope and optimism.

And then, you want to find a job within two weeks. Or yesterday.

In any event, the question is, what should you do?

Where should you begin?

You must begin by understanding this simple truth:

THE WORKPLACE IS ALWAYS CHANGING

The workplace is always changing, always in turmoil, always in flux.

Fields rise, fall, and all but disappear. Look at farming. In 1890, 43% of all the workers in the U.S. were farmers. By 1920, that was down to 27%. By 1950, 12.2%. By 1970, 4.6%. And in 1995, only 1.9%.[1] The number of farms currently (1,925,000) is at a level not seen since 1850. Of course, at the same time new occupational fields arise, such as computing, and we begin the process all over again.

Occupations rise, fall, and all but disappear. Look at the blacksmith, the buggy-whip maker, and others. Of course, at the same time new occupations arise, such as computer animator, and we begin the process all over again.

Companies rise, fall, and often disappear. Remember Gimbels, Wanamakers, The New York Sun, I. Magnin's, the *Saturday*

---

1. *U.S.A. Today*, April 8, 1996.

Review, Kresge's, any number of steel companies, and others? Gone. Of course, at the same time new companies arise, such as Netscape, and older companies redesign and reshape themselves, with new strategies, new technology, and new products or services, and thus we begin the process all over again.

It follows from all of this that *jobs* also rise, fall, and often disappear. Look at the hostile takeovers, mergers, downsizing, and other trends which have caused so many jobs to disappear in the last few years. Of course, at the same time new jobs are born, at least two million of them a year (on average) in the U.S., often in other fields, and we begin the process all over again.

Yes, the workplace is always in flux, always in transition, always in turmoil -- it always has been, and it always will be.

So, in the '90s the workplace is just doing what it has always done. But there *are* six things that are different about the '90s:

First of all, this normal process of change and flux has been greatly speeded up, much like the 'time-lapse' photography you sometimes see on TV, where the clouds seem to race across the sky. They've thought of a dozen names for this *speeded-up process*: merging, downsizing, restructuring, rightsizing, reengineering, delayering, reorganizing, consolidating etc. They all refer to the speeding up of a normal process in the job-market.

Secondly, what is different about the '90s is that a larger number of workers than normal have been affected by this more rapid change. *And,* these workers come from all different classes -- even those classes which, in the *old days* seemed immune to the changes affecting everyone else -- particularly

white-collar workers, and middle to upper management. In the U.S. alone almost three million people are laid off annually, which means more than 43 million U.S. jobs have been erased since 1979. This is beyond normal. In fact, seven out of ten U.S. households have had some kind of 'close encounter' with layoffs since 1979; four out of every ten households know a relative, friend, or neighbor who was laid off; and one out of every three U.S. households has had a family member laid off.[2]

Thirdly, what is different about the '90s is that there is much less warning of anything. When the changes occur, when jobs are terminated or disappear in this decade, there may in fact be no warning at all. Some workers have learned they had no job by listening to the radio while driving to work that morning. This has greatly increased people's jitters and anxiety, in the workplace. Every new layoff causes more anxiety among those who are left.

Fourth, what is different about the '90s is that there is a great deal more injustice in the workplace. While admittedly mergers or downsizings are used by employers to get rid of employees they wished to fire anyway, it is also true that loyal, effective employees, with ten, twenty years' devoted service, are getting unjustly discharged. In too many places, these include those employees who helped make the place run well, gave it heart, and caring. They are let go because downsizings demand every employee justify his or her existence, and their contribution was hard to measure *according to the bottom line.* Thus more than one U.S. business is unwittingly, by its downsizing, turning into a machine without a heart, because it unjustly discharged the 'heart people' that every organization needs if it is to bless the earth, and be a humane workplace.

Fifth, what is different about the '90s is that we are now in a global market, and the new jobs being born in the U.S. and elsewhere are under great pressure to stay competitive with the lower wages paid elsewhere in the world. Hence, many of the new jobs being born offer lower wages than job-hunters have been accustomed to -- resulting in lower living standards for many.

---

2. *The New York Times*, March 3, 1996.

Finally, what is different about the '90s is that the workforce is increasingly dividing into a two-class society: *those who are well off,* due to inheritance, or stockholdings, or savings in their younger years, or the fact that they are currently high-skill, high-wage, high-in-demand workers; versus *those who are having trouble keeping their head above water,* due to their having no savings, or being low-skill, low-wage workers in today's economy.

The interests of these two classes often are diametrically opposed, as when one part of the society weeps at the news of higher unemployment, while another part of the society -- namely stockholders -- rejoices at the news, since this means interest rates will stay level or come down, *that they might flourish.*

Dickens put it best, for the words he once used to describe two cities now describe the workplace of the nineties: *it was the best of times, it was the worst of times.*

Best for the many corporations and other organizations now recording record profits.

Worst for the workers who have no job security anymore, because life-long jobs are almost unheard of, and, nobody's job is safe.

That's what is different about the '90s.

MUSIC TO GET DEPRESSED BY

You may already know all of this, from vivid personal experience. Your job may have been wiped out from under you without any warning whatsoever. Your boss may have told you that you were absolutely indispensable. But, that didn't save you, because your boss lost his or her job too, at the same time you lost yours -- in that merger, that takeover, that downsizing. Your job was *gone.*

And now that you face the job-hunt, *everyone* is giving you advice.

Magazines and newspapers are.

The books in the bookstore are.

The newscaster on the TV is, in a special report.

Even your friends are, and especially those who were laid off before you, and have had a very difficult time making ends meet, ever since. They will recount their detailed history to you, of what happened to them, as a depressing prophecy of what is going to happen to you as well.

Yes, you will get advice from every side, and what it will all add up to is: *you don't stand a chance. Give up . . . now! That isn't a kind world waiting for you out there, anymore. There isn't a single job out there for you to find . . . trust us, we've looked. And even if there is, it will be at a vastly reduced income for you. Take our advice, and just retreat to your bed, pull the covers over your head, and turn the electric blanket up to nine.*

All in all, a sort of *music to get depressed by.*

You will be left with the impression that you're going to be lucky in the future if you can just manage to keep body and soul together.

PAY NO ATTENTION

You must pay no attention to this advice, of course.

And you must not give up hope.

Even if you already began your job-search -- have sent out resumes (or curricula vitae[3]) by the bushel, searched want ads by the hour, and visited federal/state, and private employment agencies from A to Z, all without turning up a single thing.

This says nothing about whether or not you can find a job.

---

3. Curricula vitae (plural) or curriculum vitae (singular) is a term used in academia and in other countries than the U.S., as a synonym for *resumes.* It's abbreviated, often, to c.v.

There *is* a way. You *can* find a job, and a job which you love. You *can* flourish.

In order to understand how, let us look together at:

TWO FUNDAMENTAL TRUTHS
ABOUT THE JOB-MARKET

You may know people trapped by their inability to find anything like the work they used to have, losing their home, breaking up their marriage, never recovering the standard of living they formerly enjoyed. And if you have kindness and compassion within you, you will feel deeply the pain of these lives, wrecked by their inability to survive in today's job market.

Yet, beyond your compassion for them you of course want also to have compassion for yourself. You want to know if there is anything you can do to avoid their fate. And perhaps even help them, once you've turned your own life around.

You want to know if it is possible to conduct a job-hunt victoriously in today's vastly-changed job-market.

The answer is, *Yes, it is.* But only if you first learn, and memorize, two fundamental truths about the job-market.

These have always been true. These will always be true. They are:

> 1. There are always jobs out there.

> 2. Whether you can find them or not, depends on what methods of job-hunting you are using.

Let's begin with the first.

THERE ARE ALWAYS JOBS
OUT THERE

I will illustrate my points with U.S. statistics, but the same truths obtain, in countries around the world.

As I write, there are currently 125,163,000 people holding jobs in the U.S. One out of every 8.5 of those is self-employed.[4] That leaves 110,466,000 who work for somebody else. Now, even if the number of jobs in the U.S. were frozen at that number, and not another single job were created for some time to come, there would still be jobs available. Why?

Because people presently holding jobs get **promoted**, thus leaving vacant the job they had.

And because people get **fired** due to unsatisfactory performance on the job, thus creating vacancies.

And because people presently holding jobs **quit**, thus creating vacancies.

And because people presently holding jobs get seriously **injured**, on the job or on the road or at home, and are no longer able to come to work, thus creating vacancies.

And because people presently holding jobs develop **illnesses** requiring long hospitalizations, thus creating vacancies.

And because people presently holding jobs have to **move**, in order to be near a sick or dying relative, thus creating vacancies.

And because people reach the age where they decide to **retire**, thus creating vacancies.

And because people **die** suddenly, while still in the workforce, thus creating vacancies.

And because some of those jobs are actually **limited contracts**, and when they run out, there will be monies available for new contracts, often in those same companies.

Vacancies, then, are *always* being created -- simply because we are human. And that will never change.

---

4. According to the U.S. Department of Labor, *Monthly Labor Review*, January/ February 1996, p. 3. The Department claims that only one out of every 11 workers is self-employed, but this is because they exclude all self-employed who have incorporated their business (the Department's reasoning here is *legal:* technically self-employed people who incorporate their business thus become employees of their own businesses). However, totaling all self-employed persons, whether they have incorporated their business or not, yields the conclusion that one out of every 8.5 workers in the U.S. is self-employed.

VACANCIES EVEN DURING RECESSIONS

These 'revolving chairs' in the workforce occur even during recessions or other economic 'hard times.'

In the U.S., there have been nine recessions since World War II. During a recent recession, the National Federation of Independent Business conducted a survey to discover how many vacancies there were among small businesses. They discovered there were one and a half million, *during that recession.* And that was just for *small* businesses, never mind *large* businesses.

Sometimes, these vacancies take a *long* time to be filled. Our job-hunting system is Neanderthal. And employers are just as baffled about how to find good workers, as the unemployed are about how to find good employers.

If you can find one of these jobs while it is vacant, and you are qualified to perform it, and if you stand out in the job interview, you have as much chance as anyone of winning that job.

Whether you *can* find it, or not, depends of course on what methods you are using to search for it -- point #2 above, which we shall get to shortly. But, for now, my point: there are always jobs out there, even during recessions.

NEW JOBS BEING CREATED

All of this is true, as I said, even if no new jobs were ever created. But new jobs are always being created. Jobs that never existed previously. As I write, a net of 624,000 new jobs were created in the U.S. *last month alone,* despite over 300,000 layoffs.[5]

---

5. It should be emphasized that this figure, which the U.S. government publishes on the first Friday in each month, is a *net gain.* To illustrate, suppose in a given month 1,300,000 jobs were downsized and eliminated, but in that same month some 1,250,000 new jobs were created and successfully filled. The government will subtract 1,300,000 (lost) from 1,250,000 (gained) and report that the *net figure* for that month was 50,000 jobs lost -- implying that *no* job-hunters found a job that month -- or, as the average reader, interprets it, "there are no jobs out there." This is wrong. With my rich skills at overkill, let me repeat: there were 1,250,000 jobs found that month. From this you can see that in those months which report a large increase -- say, a *net gain* of 624,000 jobs as above -- there is actually a much larger number of job-hunters successfully finding jobs *that month* than even the figure of 624,000 would suggest.

If you want the yearly statistic, it is: during the twelve months ending February 1996, 2,566,000 new jobs were created in the U.S. (This is, I remind you, the *net* figure.)

That's a lot of new jobs. And you have as much chance as anyone of winning one of these jobs, *if* you can find them, and *if* you are qualified to perform them, and *if* you stand out in the job interview.

Whether you *can* find them, or not, depends on what methods you are using to search for them -- which we shall get to shortly. For now, my point: there are always jobs out there.

Write it on your bathroom mirror, hum it, sing it, repeat it like a litany, this refrain: there are always jobs out there. There are always jobs out there.

HOW MANY JOBS ARE THERE FOR ME TO GO AFTER?

That's a natural curiosity. It takes a little figuring, so follow this step by step *(or just skip over this section, and take my word for it):* U.S. studies have repeatedly turned up the fact that during a typical year as many as twenty percent[6] of the workforce are out of work *at some time* during that year. That would currently work out to 25 million workers who are unemployed at some time during the year. Now, the monthly unemployment rate is never around 25 million. It's around 8 million.

So, obviously, sometime during the year, 17 million unemployed people were able *to find a new job before the year ended.*[7]

To be sure, some of these jobs are new jobs in places and fields that the job-hunters-in-question would have preferred to turn down, so that they could go find some new place which would let them do their old jobs again.

---

6. The first source of this figure is The Conference Board, 1991. A Time/CNN poll put it even higher, at 23% ("23% of American workers were unemployed, not by their own choice, at some time in 1991" *Time,* January 13, 1992). The yearly count has been taken by the U.S. government over a number of years, and in good times or bad it seems to always work out that approximately one out of every five people in the workforce is unemployed *sometime* during any given year.

7. The figure of 17 is arrived at by subtracting 8 from 25.

Also, some of those jobs are part-time, when the job-hunters-in-question would have preferred them to be full-time.

And some of those jobs pay lower wages when they would have liked them to pay higher wages.

And some of these jobs are temporary, when the job-hunters-in-question would have liked them to be -- *I dare not say* permanent, *because I believe hardly any jobs are permanent anymore, in this new world economy* -- but, yes, they would have liked them to last at least a few years, maybe more. That's 'permanent' in today's economy.

Well, you get my point. The quality of the work found isn't always up to snuff; nonetheless, each year *millions* of people become unemployed, and then successfully find jobs.

There is no reason why you should not be among them. And no reason why you should not aim to find the very best job you can imagine, even if it later turns out that you have to get to it in two or three steps. In good times or bad, there are *always* jobs out there. *Say it again, Sam.*

THEY'RE OUT THERE, BUT CAN YOU FIND THEM?

> 2. Whether you can find them or not, depends on what methods of job-hunting you are using.

We come now to our second fundamental truth about the job market.

How do you find the jobs that are out there, waiting for you to find them?

Well, you say, *if they're out there, it should be easy to find them.* No, no, no, mon ami. That is not the case.

To illustrate this, let us step outside the world of work for a moment, and let us take an example from personal life.

Suppose you moved to a big city, and found a really nice apartment to rent, but you decided you didn't want (or need) a telephone. And now let us suppose that some months later someone over on the other side of that city is asked if you live there. They've never heard of you, so their first response is, "I dunno." *(An English major, obviously.)* Being resourceful, they go and look in the telephone book, because they assume that *anyone* who lives in the big city *must* have a telephone. But when they look, there is no mention of you. They call information to ask if you have an unlisted number. Nope.

So, what do they conclude? They conclude you don't exist -- at least not in that city. And why did they reach this conclusion? Because they thought the way to find you was through the telephone book, and in that, they were quite wrong.[8]

Mark the main point of my little illustration. The fact that you exist does not automatically mean you are easy to find. Normal methods for locating you may not work.

And so it is with the job-hunt. The fact that a job exists does not automatically mean it is easy to find. Normal methods for locating it may not work.

You know what I mean by *normal methods,* of course: the ones we all turn to -- resumes, want-ads, and employment agencies.

The job you most want to find may be out there, waiting for you to come find it; yet resumes, want-ads, and employment agencies cannot turn it up. You need to know about other methods. I have listed them all, here, together with their estimated success rate, based on studies of actual job-hunters after they found -- or didn't find -- a job.[9]

---

8. Now, lest you think I am downplaying the phone book in general, let me mention that in job-hunting the telephone book is a lifesaver, particularly The Yellow Pages, as you will see, later. Don't let such details make you forget the overarching point of my parable, which is: choose one method to try to find somebody, and you may strike out . . . even though they're *there.*

9. Since my tips and suggestions rest heavily on what successful job-hunters did, you may have an idle curiosity to know where these studies are to be found. Their sources are:

Steven M. Bortnick and Michelle Harrison Ports, "Job search methods and results: tracking the unemployed, 1991," *Monthly Labor Review,* December 1992. Studied the success of job-seekers who had been looking for a job, over a period of 8 weeks.

THE FIVE WORST WAYS
TO TRY TO FIND THOSE JOBS
THAT ARE OUT THERE

1. Mailing out **resumes** to employers at random. *This method has a 7% success rate -- that is, out of every 100 job-hunters who use this method, 7 will find a job thereby.*

93 job-hunters out of 100 will not find the jobs that *are* out there -- if they use only this method.

(*One study revealed there is only one job-offer for every 1470 resumes floating around out there; another study puts the figure even higher -- one job offer for every 1700 resumes floating around out there. Would you take an airplane, if you knew only one out of 1700 got through, to their destination?*)

2. Answering **ads in professional or trade journals**, appropriate to your field. *This method also has a 7% success rate -- that is, out of every 100 job-hunters who use this method, 7 will find a job thereby.*

93 job-hunters out of 100 will not find the jobs that *are* out there -- if they use only this method.

3. Answering **non-local newspaper ads**, in other parts of the state or country. *This method has a 10% success rate -- that is, out of every 100 job-hunters who use this method, 10 will find a job thereby.*

90 job-hunters out of 100 will not find the jobs that *are* out there -- if they use only this method.

John Bishop, John Barron and Kevin Hollenbeck, *Recruiting Workers: How recruitment policies affect the flow of applicants and quality of new workers.* The Ohio State University, The National Center for Research in Vocational Education, Sept. 1983. They discovered that "informal search methods" (such as described here in *Parachute*) are more effective than "formal search methods," such as employment agencies.

Carl Rosenfeld, "Job Search of the Unemployed, May 1976," *Monthly Labor Review,* November 1977. A Bureau of Labor Statistics study, which - - unlike the first study cited above - - interviewed job-hunters at only one moment in time.

Bureau of the Census, "Use and Effectiveness of Job Search Methods," *Occupational Outlook Quarterly,* Winter, 1976. A study of ten million job-seekers.

4. Answering local **newspaper ads**. *This method has a 5–24% success rate -- that is, out of every 100 job-hunters who use this method, between 5 and 24 will find a job thereby.*

76–95 job-hunters out of 100 will not find the jobs that *are* out there -- if they use only this method.

(The fluctuation in range is due to the level of salary that is being sought; the higher the salary being sought, the fewer job-hunters who are able to find a job using this method).

5. Going to **private employment agencies** for help. *This method also has a 5–24% success rate, again, depending on the level of salary that is being sought -- which is to say, out of every 100 job-hunters who use this method, between 5 and 24 will find a job thereby.*

76–95 job-hunters out of 100 will not find the jobs that *are* out there -- if they use only this method.

(It should be noted that the success rate of this method has risen slightly in recent years, in the case of women but not of men: in a recent study, 27.8% of female job-hunters found a job within two months, by going to private employment agencies.)[10]

Well, as we noted earlier, there are always jobs out there, waiting to be found. But, the methods just described are the five *least* effective ways of locating them.

---

10. There are at least four other methods for trying to find the jobs that are out there, which fall neither into the "Five Least Effective" category, nor into the "Five Most Effective" category. These are:

a. Going to **places where employers pick out workers**. This has an 8% success rate -- that is, out of every 100 people who use this method, 8 will find a job thereby. 92 will not. (15% of U.S. workers are union members, and it is claimed that those among them who have access to a union hiring hall, have a 22% success rate -- that is, 22 out of every 100 find a job using this method. What is not stated, however, is how long it takes to get a job at the hall, and how long a job typically lasts-- in the trades, that may be for just a few days.)

b. Taking **a Civil Service examination**. This has a 12% success rate -- that is, out of every 100 people who use this method, 12 will find a job thereby. 88 will not.

c. Asking **a former teacher or professor** for job-leads. This also has a 12% success rate -- that is, out of every 100 people who use this method, 12 will find a job thereby. 88 will not.

d. Going to **the state/Federal employment service office**. This has a 14% success rate -- that is, out of every 100 people who use this method, 14 will find a job thereby. 86 will not.

I'm sure you noticed that our old friends -- resumes, ads, and agencies -- all appear on this Five *Worst* List.

So, if you use resumes, ads, and agencies to find a job, but they turn up *nothing*, it doesn't mean there are no jobs out there. It only means *those methods* can't find them. Sorry about that.

It's time to learn some new ways of finding the jobs that are out there. This brings us to:

THE FIVE BEST WAYS
TO TRY TO FIND THOSE JOBS
THAT ARE OUT THERE

1. **Asking for job-leads** from family members, friends, people in the community, staff at career centers -- especially at your local community college or the high-school or college where you graduated. You ask them one simple question: do you know of any jobs where you work -- or elsewhere? *This method has a 33% success rate -- that is, out of every 100 people who use this method, 33 will find a job thereby.*

67 job-hunters out of 100 will not find the jobs that *are* out there -- if they use only this method.

2. **Knocking on the door of any employer, factory, or office that interests you,** whether they are known to have a vacancy

or not. *This method has a 47% success rate -- that is, out of every 100 people who use this method, 47 will find a job thereby.*

53 job-hunters out of 100 will not find the jobs that *are* out there -- if they use only this method.

3. **By yourself, using the phone book's Yellow Pages** to identify subjects or fields of interest to you in the town or city where you are, and then calling up the employers listed in that field, to ask if they are hiring for the type of position you can do, and do well. *This method has a 69% success rate that is, out of every 100 job-hunters or career-changers who use this method, 69 will find a job thereby.*

31 job-hunters out of 100 will not find the jobs that *are* out there -- if they use only this method.

4. **In a group with other job-hunters, using the phone book's Yellow Pages** to identify subjects or fields of interest to you in the town or city where you are, and then calling up the employers listed in that field, to ask if they are hiring for the type of position you can do, and do well. *This method has an 84% success rate -- that is, out of every 100 people who use this method, 84 will find a job thereby.*

16 job-hunters out of 100 will not find the jobs that *are* out there -- if they use only this method.

5. *The Creative Approach to Job-Hunting or Career-Change.* This can be done by individuals, or in groups. The characteristics of this system, in general, are: *Do thorough homework, and inventory, upon yourself. Know your favorite skills, in their order of priority. Know in what kinds of fields you want to use those skills. Talk to people who are in those kind of jobs. Find out if they like their job, and how they found their job. Then choose organizations where you want to work, rather than just those* known *to have vacancies. Do research on the organizations, thoroughly, before approaching them. Seek out the person who actually has the power to hire you for the job you want; use your personal contacts and friends to get in to see him or her. Show them how you can help them with their problems.* Cut no corners, take no shortcuts. This method is explained completely in the chapters entitled, *For the Determined Job-Hunter. This method has an 86% success rate -- that is, out of every 100 job-hunters*

or career-changers who use this method, 86 will find a job or new career thereby.

14 job-hunters out of 100 will not find the jobs that *are* out there -- if they use only this method.

"WHILE YOU'RE WAITING FOR YOUR SHIP
TO COME IN, WHY DON'T YOU DO SOME
MAINTENANCE WORK ON THE PIER ?"

WHAT IF YOU USE
MORE THAN ONE METHOD?

Ah, how brilliant you are, to have thought of that! Thanks to the studies that have been done, we happen to know the answer. In general, as you might suspect, the answer is that the greater the number of job-hunting methods any job-hunter uses, the greater his or her success at finding a job. That fact was uncovered in a study that was done over 25 years ago.[11] Makes sense, doesn't it?

But, a more recent study, published four years ago, uncovered this strange twist: it is true that the likelihood of your uncovering those jobs that are always out there *increases* with each additional method that you use, but only *up to four.* If you use

---

11. The study was made a number of years ago, in Erie Pennsylvania, by A. Harvey Belitsky and Harold L. Sheppard. It was published under the title *The Job Hunt: Job-Seeking Behavior of Unemployed Workers in a Local Economy* (now out of print). A summary of it was published by The W.E. Upjohn Institute for Employment Research, 300 South Westnedge Ave., Kalamazoo MI 49007, called *Promoting Jobfinding Success for the Unemployed* (now also out of print). Originally, I did much of my own research on job-hunting when this Institute kindly gave me an office at their Washington D.C. offices. What remains of that Institute is now located only in Kalamazoo.

more than four methods, your likelihood of uncovering those jobs that are out there, starts to *decrease*.[12]

I have pondered this bizarre finding, and concluded that the explanation may lie in the fact that if you try to do more than four methods you will end up not doing any of them very well. You will give each method less time than it deserves and needs, if it is to be effective.

DON'T JUST USE
ONE METHOD

Well, then, why not use just one job-hunting method, and do it exceptionally well?

The answer lies in the fact that in the U.S. as well as other countries the job-hunt typically lasts two to four months, *and* one-third of all job-hunters never find a job because they *give up* during that time. Often, of course, the job-hunt lasts far longer -- from six months to two years or more -- and many more job-hunters don't find a job, simply because they abandon their job-hunt.[13] Job-hunting demands persistence, and stick-to-it-ive-ness.

So, why do we give up? I mean, we need that income, don't we? Why do we give up?

It turns out the 'why' is related to the number of methods you use. For example, studies have discovered that out of every 100 job-hunters who use only one method of job-search, 51 of them abandon their search, by the second month.

On the other hand, out of every 100 job-hunters who use *several* job-search methods, only 31 abandon their search, by the second month.[14] The logic seems to be that if you use only one method -- say, resumes -- and it doesn't turn up anything rather quickly, you tend to give up hope. But if you are using two, three, or four methods, your hope tends to stay alive --

12. Steven M. Bortnick and Michelle Harrison Ports, "Job search methods and results: tracking the unemployed, 1991," *Monthly Labor Review,* December 1992, p. 33.

13. "How Long Does Unemployment Last?" by the late Robert G. Wegmann, *The Career Development Quarterly,* September 1991. The median for unemployed workers in the U.S. was 13.7 weeks in 1994; currently as I write, 1,300,000 U.S. job-hunters have been unemployed for 27 weeks or longer.

14. Steven M. Bortnick and Michelle Harrison Ports, "Job search methods and results: tracking the unemployed, 1991," *Monthly Labor Review,* December 1992.

surely, one of these will pay off -- and so, you keep on looking.

The moral of our tale, then, is this: avoid using just one job-search method, because it will lead quickly to discouragement, if it doesn't pay off almost immediately. The experience of successful job-hunters is that you should use more than one method, though not more than four.

Beyond numbers, you want of course to choose one or more of these from the Five *Best* List, above -- and not pick *all* of them from the Five *Worst* List. *(Among the Five* Worst, *stand resumes* -- *and I am assuming you will not give up that misplaced faith in their effectiveness, no matter what I tell you. Okay, okay. Just be sure to supplement them with one or more methods from the Five* Best *List.)*

SUMMARY

Most job-hunters, and career-changers, believe that whatever job-hunting method they use, if there are jobs out there, they will find them.

But in fact, studies of successful and unsuccessful job-hunters have revealed that *everything* depends on what method or methods you are using.

> There are always jobs, waiting to be filled. The successful job-hunter is the one who knows how to find them.
>
> Successful job-hunting is a learned skill. It can be studied. It can be mastered. By You.
>
> This book is dedicated to teaching you that skill.

If you use a relatively ineffective method, and it turns up nothing, you will, of course, say to yourself, Well, there are no jobs. But the truth is: yes there are; you are simply using the wrong method for finding them *(hint: resumes don't cut it!).*

You must use an effective method, and in fact, if you are to stick with your job-hunt, you should consider using at least two effective methods, though not more than four, for thus you keep hope alive. With hope, you can persist until you find what you are looking for.

*"It ain't what you don't know
that gets you in trouble;
it's what you know for sure
that ain't so."*

Mark Twain

FOR THE IMPATIENT JOB-HUNTER

QUICK STRATEGIES

47 TIPS, HINTS, SHORTCUTS

Chapter 3

Table of Contents

What makes us become impatient with the job-hunt?

Well, for one thing, it lasts too long. Many years, the U.S. job-hunt typically lasts around 100 days. It can be much shorter than that, but alas! it can also be much longer -- many times longer. Six months. A year. Two years.

And . . . one-third of all job-hunters never find a job because they *give up* during the first months -- especially if they were using only one method, such as resumes, to locate the jobs that are out there.[1]

No wonder we so easily become The Impatient Job-Hunter. "Let's get this over with!"

And then our grumpiness grows. We know the jobs are out there, but why do we have to go *hunting* for them? Why doesn't somebody just hand us one of them?

We wish someone would save us from this hunt. We want someone to *rescue* us, come after us, offer us work: *"Here, here's a job; take it. It's for you!"* Save us all that *huntin'*, and blood, sweat, and tears.

We're a little vague about who that someone should be: the government perhaps, or our previous employer (who, after

---

1. "How Long Does Unemployment Last?" by the late Robert G. Wegmann, *The Career Development Quarterly*, September 1991. The median for unemployed workers in the U.S. was 13.7 weeks in 1994; currently as I write, 1,300,000 U.S. job-hunters have been unemployed for 27 weeks or longer.

all, *owes* us), or the unions. But we expect rescue. We wait for rescue.

And it does not come.

The hard truth is this: no one owes you a job, no matter what your family or friends may have told you; if you want a job, it is you who is going to have to go out, and work hard to find it.

WHO ARE THE JOB-HUNTING EXPERTS?

If you don't know how to find a job, there is a simple remedy to accelerate and speed up your learning: go talk to *successful* job-hunters among your family, friends, and acquaintances -- people who *were* out of work, and since then have found a job they really love -- and learn what *they* did. Then go imitate it. If you do that, you can probably throw away this book.

This is, after all, how you master *anything*. If you play tennis, and you want to learn how to improve your game, you go talk to, or train with, *good* tennis players, to learn how they do it. If you run, and want to improve your running, you would go talk to, or train with, *good* runners, and learn how they do it. If you paint, and want to learn how to paint better, you would go study under *master* painters, to see how they do it.

It is the same with job-hunting. If you are job-hunting, and you want to learn how to do it better, talk to people who are good at it.

Of course, you may not know that many successful job-hunters, in your circle of acquaintances. Which is why you have this book in your hand. You are hoping that I do. Ah yes. I know *thousands* and *thousands* of them. And, in the remainder of this chapter, I want to share with you a number of hints, tips, shortcuts, and quick strategies for the impatient job-hunter, that I have learned from them, during the last twenty-five years and more.

Needless to say *(but I'll say it, anyway)*, none of these tips can *guarantee* you a job. Life can never be so mechanized. There is always so much in life that depends on luck and chance and serendipity. But if faithfully followed, these ideas should at least dramatically *improve* your chances of finding a job more quickly, as so many successful job-hunters have discovered, before you.

Tips
About the Job-Hunt
In General

★ You will have to job-hunt many times in your life.

★ It will be an average of eight times, in each U.S. worker's lifetime.

★ It may be as often as every three years.

★ You must master the job-hunt for yourself, this time, so that the next time you go about it, you will know how to do it.

★ Most people make career decisions on the flimsiest of grounds, justifying the root meaning of the word *career*, which comes from *careen* -- to go around the ancient Roman race-track at top speed, in a precipitous headlong rush.

★ There are three parts to every job-hunt or career-change: What, Where, and How. You need to learn techniques, to help you do each part.

★ More important than techniques, however, is your attitude toward your job-hunt. Attitude is *everything!*

"We who lived in concentration camps can remember the men who walked through the huts comforting others, giving away their last piece of bread. They may have been few in number, but they offer sufficient proof that every-thing can be taken from a man but one thing: the last of the human freedoms -- to choose one's attitude in any given set of circumstances . . . "

Victor Frankl

Attitude is a matter of: Your attitude toward the job-hunt. Your attitude toward the employer. Your attitude toward the job. Believe me, your attitude is the first (and last) thing every-one notices about you.

It is hardly any surprise, therefore, that when asked why they didn't hire *so and so*, employers invariably reply, "He had a real *attitude* problem." *Or* "I didn't like her attitude." *Or* "I thought he had a lousy attitude."

For the impatient job-hunter, anxious to find a job as quickly as possible, attitude is the first thing that must be looked at and (if necessary) fixed.

GENERAL ATTITUDE

Attitude is, first of all a matter of how you come across to people, in your personality. It is the first thing that every employer notices about you, during a job-interview, *or even earlier -- in telephone contact, or resume.*

Attitude is the killer question about you, that dances like sugarplums in every employer's head.[2] They notice, immediately, whether you would be a pleasant person to be around, or not. They notice, immediately, whether you are interested in other people, their interests and needs, or totally absorbed with yourself. Whether you project energy and enthusiasm, or minimal effort and sullenness. Whether you are angry, or at peace with yourself and the world. Outgoing, or turned in on yourself. Communicative, or monosyllabic. Interested in giving, or only in taking. Anxious to do the best job possible, going the extra mile, or anxious to 'just go through the motions.'

Employers will hire someone with lesser skills, who has the right attitude, rather than a more-skilled person with a bad attitude. They have had enough experience with bad attitudes in the past, to know that if they were foolish enough to hire you, and you turn out to have a bad attitude, they will soon ache to get rid of you. That is why they are supersensitive to your attitude, from the first moment they lay eyes on you.

YOUR ATTITUDE TOWARD TODAY'S JOB MARKET

From general attitude, we progress to *specific*. Employers are sensitive to how you are dealing with the world as it is, today . . . not the world you wish existed.

---

2. Or, if you are self-employed, this dances in every one of your potential clients' heads.

If you have been unjustly let go at your previous job, your first great need is to let go of your righteous anger at how different the world of work is from what you thought it would be; otherwise, that anger will cripple your job-hunting efforts. You will reek of it to every employer you go see, even as a drunk reeks of strong drink.

You may love or hate what's happened to the job market in the '90s, and what it's done to your life. But you've got to make your peace with it. In this arena, as in others, your attitude is *crucial,* and every employer will notice it.

Okay, so, how should you mentally prepare yourself for today's job market? There are four attitudes I think are crucial to the success of your job-hunt:

• **1. Every job you get is temporary.** *That is, 'of uncertain length.' 90% of the workforce in the U.S. is* not *self-employed; so, you are probably going to end up working for someone else. And how long that job lasts will be up to them, and not just you. If they so will it, your job may end at any time, and without warning.* You are always 'on probation,' as is the company you are working for. The question is: are you ready for the next job when this one fails?

This is the *nature of today's job market. So, when you go job-hunting, you must think to yourself, "I am hunting for a job that is basically a temporary job, whose length I do not know. Therefore, this is not going to be my last job-hunt, in all likelihood. I'm going to have to be mentally prepared to start job-hunting again, at any time."*

It is helpful for you to have the attitude, before you start your job-hunt, that whatever job you find is going to be treated by you as a temporary job, which may end at any time. This has always been true to some degree, but now it is even more true than ever.

As a preparation for this attitude in the future, write down, on a separate piece of paper, how long each job has lasted, throughout your work history.

• **2. Every job you get is essentially a seminar**. The question is: what are you learning there?

Of course you want this job to put bread on the table, clothes on your back, and a roof over your head. And, you want it to give you a sense of satisfaction and accomplishment. But. Almost every job today is moving and changing so fast, in its very nature, that you must think of this job you are looking for, as one that will inevitably be a learning experience for you. Think of it as enrolling in a seminar. There is a lot you will have to learn . . . when you begin . . . and throughout the time you are there. You must not only be ready to learn, but eager to learn. You must emphasize to every would-be employer how much you love to learn new tasks and procedures, and how fast you learn.

It is helpful for you to have the attitude, before you start your job-hunt, that whatever job you find is going to be treated by you as a seminar, and learning experience. This has always been true to some degree, but now it is even more true than ever.

As a preparation for this attitude in the future, write down, on a separate piece of paper, what you have learned at your present or most recent job/seminar.

• **3. Every job you get is essentially an adventure.** *Most of us love adventures. An adventure is a series of unfolding events that were unpredictable. That's today's jobs, all right! You never know what's going to happen next. If you end up working in an organization of any size, it is very likely that the dramas which will be played out there, monthly, will rival any soap opera that is on television today. Power plays! Ambition! Rumors! Poor decisions! Strange alliances! Betrayals!*

Rewards! Sudden twists and turns that no one could have predicted ahead of time, will unfold before your very eyes. Sometimes you'll love the way it is turning out; sometimes you'll hate it!

But, it is helpful for you to have the attitude, before you start your job-hunt, that whatever job you find is going to be treated by you as an adventure. This has always been true to some degree, but now it is even more true than ever.

> As a preparation for this attitude in the future, write down, on a separate piece of paper, what were the adventures -- unpredictable turns of events -- that happened to you in your present or most recent job.

• **4. Every job you get is one where the satisfaction must lie in the work itself.** *In the old days, most of us hoped we would find not only work we enjoyed, but also appreciation and recognition for that work. In other words, we looked for a kind of love at our place of work. Well, there are indeed such places still out there, where you can be appreciated, saluted, singled-out and praised to the skies -- but they are not as common or as easy to find, as they used to be -- particularly if the organization has over 50 employees.*

Despite your best research during your job-hunt, you may end up in a job where your bosses fail to recognize or acknowledge the fine contribution that you make, leaving you feeling unloved and unappreciated -- and finally, even after many months or years, they may let you go, and without warning, citing a business turn-down, the need for 'new blood,' bankruptcy, merger, or the full-moon.

So consider how urgent it is, in today's job market, that your attitude should be: "I am going to choose a job which feeds my self-esteem by the very doing of it, rather than settling for work which has no satisfaction unless I receive praise from my supervisors."

It has always been true, but now it is more true than ever: before you start job-hunting, you *must* spend as much care as you possibly can, on defining carefully for yourself what kind of job(s) would give you great pleasure in the very doing of it; pleasure because:

    you get to use the skills you most love to use,
    in the field you most love to work in,

toward those goals you would most love to accomplish,
knowing that God knows what an asset you are to that place,
even when your employers don't.

> As a preparation for this attitude in the future, write down,
> on a separate piece of paper, what were the satisfactions
> that you got out of your present or most recent job.

MORE THAN JUST A JOB-HUNT

You can choose to go reluctantly, or gladly, into today's job market. If you go reluctantly -- if you demand that your next job should give you permanence, predictability, and no need to learn anything new -- then your job-hunt may turn out to be very difficult indeed, where you end up settling for just the most boring of jobs.

But if you love learning, if you love adventure, if you love finding satisfaction in the work itself, and if you can handle a job's uncertain length, then you can go job-hunting gladly, as this will be more than just a job-hunt.

It will be a hunt for new ways to learn. It will be a hunt for adventure. And it will be a hunt for the skills you most love to use, in the field where you most love to use them. And it will be a full-time job, in itself.

And now, we move on, from *attitude*, to 47 tips, hints, and shortcuts dealing with the three parts of a job-hunt:

Tips

About Deciding WHAT You Would Like to Do

☆ Do not expect that you will necessarily be able to find exactly the same kind of work that you used to be doing. Oh, I know what you're thinking. If you enjoyed your last job, you're thinking: *"I would like to look for exactly the kind of work I used to do, in the past, with the same exact job-title."*

And maybe you can. *But,* be prepared for the fact that in this changing life, and changing world, jobs do vanish. You must not necessarily expect that you will be able to find exactly the same kind of work that you did in the past. So, you need to take the job-label off yourself (*"I am an auto-worker,"* etc.) and define yourself instead as *"I am a person who . . . "*

Define some other line (or lines) of work that you could do, can do, and would enjoy doing.

2

☆ Forget about "vacancies." Go after the job you really want the most.

3

☆ Maybe you already know what that is. Ask yourself this question: *what is it in the world that I'd love to do more than anything else?* Whose job that you see *out there* -- among all the people you've met, know, or read about -- would you most love to be able to do? You may be able to describe this right off the top of your head; perhaps something you've already done, in your spare time (*like: make dresses, repair sailboats, etc.*)

4

☆ Maybe you don't know what the job is, that you'd most love to do. In that case, there is a simple rule: **don't decide on your future, until you have first inventoried your past** (get out a pad of paper, and a pencil -- or, go to your computer, and list some answers to these questions):

"What have I done in the past that I really loved doing?" (Hobbies, spare time activities, and volunteer work?)

"What *did* I like about these things? What do I *still* like doing?"

"What am I good at? What does everyone tell me?"

"What would I love to sell, if I *had to* make a living as a salesperson?"

5

☆ Ask yourself simple questions, for example, whether you primarily like to use your Skills with People, or your Skills with Things, or your Skills with Information. As someone has said, the point of all career planning is to simplify the things you know about yourself, and pick out those few elements that give you your power in life.

6

☆ What are you sensitive to, that you don't think everybody necessarily is? This could be things your eyes pick up (e.g., colors, facial expressions, bodies showing injury); *or* things your ears pick up (e.g., birdsongs); *or* things your nose picks up (e.g., faint odors in the air); *or* things your mouth picks up (e.g., peculiar tastes); *or* things your body picks up (e.g., air currents, temperature changes); *or* things your brain picks up (e.g., connections, disharmony, remembering details), etc., etc. What kinds of jobs would use this sensitivity?

7

☆ What turns you on? If a thing turns you on, you'll be good at it; if it doesn't, you won't. (*This hint courtesy of David Maister.*)

8

☆ What exhausts you? What energizes you? Go for the work, and tasks, that energize you. What are your hobbies? Astronomy? Aerospace? Airplanes? Bicycling? Birding? Boating or kayaking? Books? Cars? Caves? Collecting coins, or stamps, or dolls, or anything else? Cooking? Crafts? Dance? Electronics? Fishing? Flowers or gardening? Genealogy? Horses? Hunting? Juggling? Magic? Martial arts or other physical stuff? Minerals or rocks? Models? Motorcycles? The outdoors? Pets? Photography? Puppetry? Trains? Travel? Woodworking? Or what? See what kinds of jobs any of these might point to, for you.

9

☆ What is, or what do you want to be, your gift to the world?

10

☆ What is it about the world that you hate the most, and would most love to help eradicate, correct or fix? How could your gifts plug into the doing of that? What is the product or service that you think your community really needs?

11

☆ What do you want out of life?

12

☆ What are your best (and favorite) skills? If you haven't a clue, following is a sampler of skill-verbs. The way in which this list is typically used by job-hunters or career-changers is to put a *separate* check mark in front of each skill that: a) you believe you possess. And a separate check mark in front of each skill that: b) you enjoy doing. And a separate check mark in front of each skill that: c) you believe you do well.

Thus a skill could end up with three check marks -- and

A List of 246 Skills as Verbs

achieving	detailing	handling	meeting	raising	studying
acting	detecting	having	memorizing	reading	summarizing
adapting	determining	responsibility	mentoring	realizing	supervising
addressing	developing	heading	modeling	reasoning	supplying
administering	devising	helping	monitoring	receiving	symbolizing
advising	diagnosing	hypothesizing	motivating	recommending	synergizing
analyzing	digging	identifying	navigating	reconciling	synthesizing
anticipating	directing	illustrating	negotiating	recording	systematizing
arbitrating	discovering	imagining	observing	recruiting	taking
arranging	dispensing	implementing	obtaining	reducing	taking
ascertaining	displaying	improving	offering	referring	instructions
assembling	disproving	improvising	operating	rehabilitating	talking
assessing	dissecting	increasing	ordering	relating	teaching
attaining	distributing	influencing	organizing	remembering	team-building
auditing	diverting	informing	originating	rendering	telling
budgeting	dramatizing	initiating	overseeing	repairing	tending
building	drawing	innovating	painting	reporting	testing and
calculating	driving	inspecting	perceiving	representing	proving
charting	editing	inspiring	performing	researching	training
checking	eliminating	installing	persuading	resolving	transcribing
classifying	empathizing	instituting	photographing	responding	translating
coaching	enforcing	instructing	piloting	restoring	traveling
collecting	establishing	integrating	planning	retrieving	treating
communicating	estimating	interpreting	playing	reviewing	trouble-
compiling	evaluating	interviewing	predicting	risking	shooting
completing	examining	intuiting	preparing	scheduling	tutoring
composing	expanding	inventing	prescribing	selecting	typing
computing	experimenting	inventorying	presenting	selling	umpiring
conceptualizing	explaining	investigating	printing	sensing	understanding
conducting	expressing	judging	problem	separating	understudying
conserving	extracting	keeping	solving	serving	undertaking
consolidating	filing	leading	processing	setting	unifying
constructing	financing	learning	producing	setting-up	uniting
controlling	fixing	lecturing	programming	sewing	upgrading
coordinating	following	lifting	projecting	shaping	using
coping	formulating	listening	promoting	sharing	utilizing
counseling	founding	logging	proof-reading	showing	verbalizing
creating	gathering	maintaining	protecting	singing	washing
deciding	generating	making	providing	sketching	weighing
defining	getting	managing	publicizing	solving	winning
delivering	giving	manipulating	purchasing	sorting	working
designing	guiding	mediating	questioning	speaking	writing

these, in fact, are the ones you want to look the hardest at, to see what kind of job they suggest.

If none of this works for you, and you just can't think of any-thing you'd really like to do, off the top of your head (or the tip of your tongue), then turn to the *Parachute Workbook,* in *The Parachute Resource Guide,* p. *7,* and do the exercises there.

13

☆ Actually, the major issue you will face with employers, vis-à-vis your skills, is not which ones you have, but how you use them: whether you just try to *keep busy,* or try to actually solve problems, thus increasing your effectiveness and the or-ganization's effectiveness, too.

14

☆ What problems could your skills help solve for an em-ployer? For example, would your skills help an employer with: making customers want to return, the quality of service, the quality of the merchandise, the timeliness of deliveries, bring-ing costs down, inventing new products, *or what?*

15

☆ Spend some time considering what makes you stand out from nineteen other people who could do the same job you can do. It will usually be a matter of *style*. Do you do it more thoroughly, faster, or what? The more you can answer this question, in a job interview, the better your chances of being the one who gets hired, instead of the other nineteen. Don't expect an employer to figure that out, for you. Be prepared to say, however modestly, *This is what makes me stand out.*

Tips
About Deciding WHERE
You Would Like to Do It

The next part of *every* job-hunt must be the question of *Where*. *Where* would you like to do it?

It makes a big difference *where* you do your favorite tasks. Everyone knows that the difference between working in an outdoor nursery, or at a law firm, is night and day.

Where you do your favorite tasks is partly a matter of what "field" you choose to work in. Hence, the questions you should be asking yourself (and jotting down the answers to) are:

16

☆ What are your favorite interests? *(Computers? Gardening? Spanish? Law? Physics? Department stores? Hospitals? etc., etc.)*

17

☆ If you just can't think of any favorite interest, ask yourself if you could talk about *something* with someone all day long, day after day, what would that subject or field of interest be?

If you were stuck on a desert island with a person who only had the capacity to speak on a few subjects, what would you pray those subjects were?

If you turn out to have more than one favorite subject, take two of them at a time, and ask yourself: if you were in a conversation with someone covering two of your favorite subjects at once, which way would you steer the conversation? Toward what subject?

18

☆ Once you know what fields interest you, look back at your answers to *What,* and see if you can put the two of them together, in terms of a particular job. For example, if you love to work with figures, and your favorite field is hospitals, you would want to think about working in the accounting department at a hospital.

19

☆ Once you have some idea of what jobs interest you, go visit places where those jobs are, and talk to people doing those jobs, to see if this *really* interests you, or not. This is called "informal research" or (sometimes) "informational interviewing."

20

☆ If you have decided to try to stay with your old career *(which you lost through downsizing or whatever)* there are ways of developing 'leads.' Ask yourself the question: *"Who might be interested in the skills and problem-solving that I learned at my last job?"*

Ask yourself who you served in your last job, or came in contact with, who might be in a position to hire someone with your talents.

Ask yourself who supplied training or staff development in your last company or field; would any of them be interested in hiring you?

Ask yourself what machines or technology you learned, mastered, improved on, at your last job; who is interested in those machines or technology?

Ask yourself what raw materials *(e.g., Kodak paper in a darkroom),* equipment, or support services you used at your last job; would any of those suppliers know of other places where their equipment or support services are used?

Ask yourself who were the subcontractors, outsourcing agencies, or temp agencies that were used at your last job; would any of them be interested in hiring you?

Ask yourself what community or service organizations were interested in your projects at your last job; would any of them be interested in hiring you? *(These suggestions courtesy of Chuck Young, Administrator for the Oregon Commission on the Blind; and Martin Kimeldorf, career counselor and author.)*

21

☆ If you have decided to try a new career (see the next chapter) or go into a new field (for you), and you are dismayed at how much preparation it looks as though it would take, go talk to people doing that work. And don't look for the rules or generalizations. Look for the exceptions to the rules. For example, everyone may tell you the rule is: *"In order to do this work you have to have a master's degree and ten years' experience at it."* But you want to find out about the exceptions. *"Yes, but do you know of anyone in the field who hasn't got all those credentials? And where might I find him or her?"*

22

☆ Once you know what kind of work you are looking for, tell everyone what it is; have as many other eyes and ears out there looking on your behalf, as possible.

23

☆ If you happen to own a telephone answering machine, you might even consider putting the kind of work you are looking for, on that machine, in your opening message: *"Hi, this is Sandra. I'm busy right now, looking for a job in the accounting department at a hospital. Leave me a message after the beep, and if you happen to have any leads or contacts for me, be sure to mention that too, along with your phone number. Thanks a lot."*

Tips
About HOW To Find The Work You're Looking For

How.

This is the final part of *any* job-hunt.

This is the most difficult part of *any* job-hunt.

After making sure you have the right *attitude* about your job-hunt in general.

After deciding *what* you are looking for,

And *where* you would like to do it,

You come to this question, which is after all the point of it all: *how* do you find such a job?

As we have seen in the previous chapter, the jobs are always out there, and some methods are much better than others for finding those jobs.

You, of course -- the Impatient Job-Hunter -- want to know how to do all of this *faster.* Okay, here are some tips.

24

☆ To speed up your search for one of the jobs that *are* out there, *you must think of yourself as having already found a job.* Your job, in this case, is that of hunting for work. Put in a larger context, think of yourself as one who always has a job. It's just that its nature varies, at different times in your life. If you were working for someone else, that was your job. If you were working for yourself, that was your job. If you are job-hunting, that is now your job. You are never without a job. Even when the world would call you 'unemployed,' you have a full-time job (without pay) from 9 to 5 every weekday, since job-hunting *is* a full-time job, just like any other in your life.

25

☆ When your job is this one -- hunting for work -- you should 'punch in' at 9, and 'punch out' at 5, just as a worker does. *You must determine to spend full-time on this phase of your hunt, if you want to speed up your job-search. Because, the swiftness with which you bring this part of your job-hunt to a successful conclusion, will be* directly *proportional to the time you spend on it.*

I emphasize this nine-to-five business, because studies have revealed the depressing fact that two-thirds of all job-hunters spend 5 hours or less hunting for a job, each week.[3] And believe me, this is true!

You must spend 35 hours a week, at least, on your search for one of the jobs that are *out there.* That should cut down, dramatically, the number of weeks it takes you to find work -- more so, than any other factor.

To illustrate, let us imagine a woman job-hunter who devotes only 5 hours a week to her search; and it turns out, in the end, to take 30 weeks, before she finds a job. That means it took a total of 150 hours.

Now let us suppose that same job-hunter were to be hurled back in time, but this time she knew it was going to take 150 hours. Therefore she decides to give 35 hours *a week* to the task, in order to 'eat up' the 150 hours faster. As you can figure out for yourself, her 150-hour job-hunt should then take only 4 weeks, or so, before she found work, other things being equal.[4]

---

3. According to the U.S. Census Bureau, discussed in "Job Search Assistance Programs: Implications for the School," authored by the late Robert G. Wegmann, and first appearing in *Phi Delta Kappan*, December 1979, pp. 271ff.

4. Of course, there are some factors beyond a job-hunter's control, that may prolong the job-hunt, such as how long it takes an interviewing-committee to schedule the next round of interviews at the place that interests you (you will often be invited back two or three times before they make up their mind about you), etc. Nonetheless, the main point of our illustration still remains.

26

☆ You must be mentally prepared (and financially prepared) for your job-hunt to last a lot longer than you think it will. *Even the shortest job-hunt still lasts between two and eighteen weeks, depending on a variety of factors, even if you work full-time at it.* It depends, of course, on what kind of job you are looking for, where you are living, how old you are, how high you are aiming, and what the state is of the local economy.

But don't count on the "two weeks" minimum. Be prepared for the eighteen weeks or longer. Experienced outplacement people have long claimed that *your search for one of the jobs that are out there* will probably take one month for every $10,000 of salary that you are seeking. This may be pure drivel, but you get the picture, don't you?

27

☆ Don't give up. Be gently, lovingly persistent about your job-hunt. One job-hunter out of every three gives up too soon. That is to say, one out of every three becomes an unsuccessful job-hunter *simply because* they abandon their search prematurely. And if you ask them why they abandoned it, they say, "I didn't think it was going to be this hard; I didn't think it was going to take this long." In other words, what 'does in' so many job-hunters is some *unspoken* mental quota in our head, which goes something like this: *I expect I'll be able to find a job after about 30 phone calls, 15 calls in person, and three interviews.* We go about our job-hunt, fill or exceed those quotas, and then give up. Without a job. At least one out of every three of us does. So, don't let this happen to you.

Keep going until you find a job. **Persistence** is the name of the game. *Persistent* means being willing to go back to places that interested you, at least a couple of times in the following months, to see if by any chance their 'no vacancy' situation has changed.

The one thing an individual needs above everything else is hope, and hope is born of persistence.

28

☆ To speed up your search for one of the jobs that *are* out there, find some kind of a support group, so that you don't have to face the job-hunt all by yourself. Ever. You'd be amazed how much the support of others can keep you going, when you might otherwise be discouraged, and thus help speed up your job-hunt. Here are the candidates you can choose from:

a. Job-hunting groups that already exist in your city or town, such as "Forty Plus" clubs, "Experience Unlimited" groups, job-hunt classes at your local Federal/state employment offices, or at the local Chamber of Commerce, or at your local college or community college, or at your local Adult Education center, or at your local church, synagogue, or place of worship.[5] The likelihood that such help is available in your community increases dramatically for you if you are from certain groups held to be disadvantaged, such as low income, or welfare recipients, or youth, or displaced workers, etc. Ask around.

b. A job-hunting group that doesn't currently exist, but that you could help form, with the aid of your priest, minister, rabbi or religious leader, at your local church, synagogue or religious center, or elsewhere -- even on the Internet. Some enterprising job-hunters, unable to locate any group, have formed their own by running an ad in the local newspaper, near the "help wanted" listings. *"Am currently job-hunting, would like to meet weekly with other job-hunters for mutual support and encouragement. Am using 'What Color Is Your Parachute?' as my guide."*

c. Your mate or partner, grandparent, brother or sister, or best friend. A loving 'taskmaster' is what you need. Someone who will make a regular weekly appointment to meet with you, check you out on what you've done that week, and be very stern with you if you've done little or nothing since you last

---

5. A U.S. listing of *some* of these kinds of places is to be found in the *National Business Employment Weekly*, on its pages called "Calendar of Career Events." It's available on many newsstands, $3.95 an issue, or you can order an issue directly from: National Business Employment Weekly, P.O. Box 300, Princeton, NJ 08543. Their phone is: 800-JOB-HUNT.

met. You want understanding, sympathy, and discipline. If your mate, brother or sister, or best friend, can offer you all of these, run -- do not walk -- to enlist them immediately.

d. A local career counselor. I grant you that career counselors aren't usually thought of as 'a support group.' But many of them do have group sessions; and even by themselves they can be of inestimable support. If you can afford their services, and none of the above suggestions have worked, this is a good fall-back strategy. Before choosing such a counselor, however, *please* read pp. *250 ff* in the *Parachute Workbook and Resource Guide,* thoroughly. That will also tell you how to locate such counselors.

29

☆ To speed up your search for one of the jobs that *are* out there, *go after many different organizations, instead of just one or two.* Restricting your search to just one or two favorite places is *death.* No matter how much you love that place, no matter how much you would *die* to work for that person, no matter how promising the situation there looks, for you (*"We'll call you next week. Promise!"*) keep on searching every day.

Don't let your job-hunt go on 'hold' just because you *hope* this place will pan out. Continue searching, at other organizations, until the day you actually begin working!!! Otherwise you will lose valuable, valuable time, when something that looked like *a sure thing* falls through, at the last moment.

Many of you will have good cause to remember these words, later, if you ignore them now!

30

☆ To speed up your search for one of the jobs that *are* out there, *determine to go after* any *place that interests you. Pay no attention to whether or not there is a known vacancy at that place.*

Underline this rule, copy it, paste it on your bathroom mirror, memorize it, repeat it to yourself every morning. I'll say it again: Pay no attention to whether or not there is a known vacancy!

If you base your job-hunt just on places where there is a known vacancy, you will prolong your search *forever!* Vacancies often develop at places *long before* any notice is put out that this vacancy exists. Moreover, when bosses or managers are thinking of creating a new position, this *intention* often lies in their mind for quite some time before they get around to doing anything about it. If you contact them during this opportune, quiescent period, you come as the answer to their prayers.

31

☆ To speed up your search for one of the jobs that *are* out there, *concentrate on organizations with twenty or less employees.* There is a natural tendency for job-hunters to make large organizations *'the measure of all things'* going on in the job-market. If the newspapers are filled with the news of companies like AT&T, General Motors, and others laying off thousands of workers, most job-hunters *assume* things are bad everywhere. This is confirmed when job-hunters focus their job-hunt only on large, well-known organizations. When they can't find a job at any of these places, they assume that *no one* is hiring. This is a very common, and very costly, mistake.

The fact is, there are always companies that are hiring -- but they are usually small companies -- with 100 or less employees. It is these which have been creating two out of every three new positions since 1970. In the U.S., for example, during the 1980s, while the Fortune 500 companies were *cutting* 3.7 million jobs from their payrolls, smaller companies *created* 19 million new jobs.[6]

So, if you would speed up your job-hunt, you need to concentrate on every *small* firm in your field that is within commuting distance, and has one hundred or less employees. Personally, I would begin with firms that have twenty or less employees.

It is true that small firms tend to have fewer benefits, such as health care, but on the other hand, they are easier to approach, the boss there is easier to get in to see, there are no forbidding personnel or human resource departments to screen you out, *and* they have the jobs.

---

6. *The San Francisco Chronicle,* 2/1/93.

You may visit any small business that interests you, but if that doesn't pay off, then go looking in particular for small businesses that are *prospering, growing, and expanding.* "The lion's share of job creation over time," says Bennett Harrison, author of *Lean and Mean: The Changing Landscape of Corporate Power in the Age of Flexibility,* "is contributed by a tiny fraction of new firms." For example, of the 245,000 businesses begun in 1985, 735 of them accounted for 75% of the employment gains between 1985 and 1988. So you are looking for businesses which may be *relatively* small now, but are on their way to *bigger.* One thinks of companies like Apple Computer which started out in a garage, or ASK Group, of Mountain View, California, which started out in a spare bedroom. Anyway, read the business section of your newspaper, daily, talk to everyone you can, talk to your Chamber of Commerce, to find out which small businesses are growing and expanding.

32

☆ To speed up your search for one of the jobs that *are* out there, *contact* at least *four employers a day, if in person; or if contacting them by telephone, forty a day, minimum; or if you're contacting them only with your resume, hundreds each week.* I emphasize this, because studies have shown that the average U.S. job-hunter only visits six employers a month. That adds up to little more than one employer *per week.*[7] That's: *visits.* Of course you can contact hundreds a week by paper (resumes); but we're talking *face-to-face.*

Logic alone will tell you that this is one of the reasons the average job-hunt takes so long. Say you were an average job-hunter, you visited only *six employers a month,* and let us say it took you *twelve months* to find a job. That means, mathematically, you had to contact 72 employers, face-to-face, in order to find that job.

But were you to be flung back in time to start all over again, except that this time you knew it will take you 72 employers, face-to-face, before you got hired, you might determine to contact, say, *four* employers *per day,* each weekday, in which case you would cover the 72 employers, and then get a job, in just a little over *three weeks,* instead of twelve months!

All of this, which you may figure out for yourself by logic, was confirmed by an actual study, which found that if a job-hunter contacted two employers a week, the job-search typically lasted up to a year; if ten employers a week, the search typically ended with a job within six months; *and,* at twenty employers a week, the search time typically dropped to 90 days or less.[8]

Therefore, common sense will tell you that you should determine to see *at least* four employers per weekday, two in the morning and two in the afternoon, at a minimum. And you should determine to do this for as many weeks (or months) as your job-hunt may last. For thus you should greatly shorten your job-hunt.

---

7. A survey cited by the late Robert G. Wegmann in "Job Search Assistance: A Review," in the *Journal of Employment Counseling,* December 1979, p. 212.

8. Goodrich & Sherwood Co., reported in "How to Succeed in Rotten Times," Oct. 1992.

When you thus approach employers, be prepared always to tell them what makes you different from nineteen other people who can do the same thing that you do. And don't be put off by rejection, if they have nothing to offer you. Be polite, ask them if they know of anyone else who might be hiring. Keep going until you find someone who is hiring.

33

☆ To speed up your search for one of the jobs that *are* out there, *use the telephone.* Some experts, of course, advise against this strategy: never, never use the telephone, they say, under *any* circumstances: it only makes it easier for the employer to screen you out over the phone.

Nonetheless, all the successful group job-search programs that I have studied over the years, from Nathan Azrin's *Job Club* to Dean Curtis's *Welfare Reform* programs *(based on the Dave Perschau/Chuck Hoffman model)* have based their programs on the *heavy* use of the telephone.

The better a group job-hunting program has worked and the faster it has succeeded in its people finding jobs, the more phone calls it has their job-hunters make. Nathan has had job-hunters make at least 10 phone calls a day; Chuck has had them make 100 phone calls in the morning, and 100 in the afternoon.

So if you've tried *everything* and all else fails, telephoning is your fall-back strategy. It is almost guaranteed to turn up something, just by its sheer weight of numbers.

Of course, I know this isn't easy -- for most of us. Some are born to it, like a duck to water. But most of us *hate* telephone solicitation, when it is directed at us; and we hate the thought of doing it ourselves, even though it is directed toward others (namely, employers).

Anyway, if you decide to do it (because you're desperate, or *really* impatient) you can go to your local library or bookstore and find books telling you exactly how to go about this.

In essence, the eleven things the experts will emphasize are these:

1. Take the Yellow Pages of the Phone Book, and call up

every single company or organization in the Yellow Pages that looks interesting to you, to ask them if they might be hiring, for the kind of work you do.

2. Write out what you plan to say. This is akin to some experts' advice that before you make your call, you should set down the objective of that call in writing before you, and the key points you want to make during the conversation. But most experts say, *Write out every word.* This is your *script*; don't try to *wing it.* Unabashedly read it, but try not to sound like you're reading it. Rehearse it first, several times.

3. If you can, start the call with a specific benefit to the caller. "I just read that you . . . and I . . ." If you can't find a connection, don't try to invent one.

4. Stand up when you make your phone calls; your voice is more forceful that way.

5. Have a mirror in front of you, on the wall, at eye level, so you can watch yourself in it, to see if you are smiling as you talk.

6. Call before 8 a.m., shortly before noon, or after 5 p.m. If it's managers you're seeking, and if they're hardworking, they're likely to be there at those times -- without a screener.

7. When you are connected, ask to speak with the manager. When she or he comes on the line, address them by name, introduce yourself by name, and then *briefly* (in one sentence) describe your greatest personal strength or top skill, a *brief* description of your experience, and then ask if there is a job opening for someone with your skills and background. For example, *"I am an experienced writer, with three published books, and I wonder if you have any job openings for someone with my experience?"* If *"yes,"* set up an interview time, repeat it, and repeat your name; if *"no,"* ask if they know of anyone else who might be hiring a person with your background. *(Courtesy of Dean Curtis.)*

8. If someone suggested you call this person, use their name as a reference when you call. "Your name was given to me by . . ."

9. If you've done something in the community, written articles for the local paper, or served on a volunteer committee, work that into the conversation if it goes on for more than one minute.

10. If you run into an interviewer's sharp objections, try responding with:

I understand . . .

I can appreciate your position . . .

I see your point . . .

Of course! However . . .

11. Some experts advise you to make fewer calls, to places that *really* interest you, and research each of them before you call. Other experts advise you not to call about a job, but to call only for information. All advise you to thank the employer before signing off, whether they have a job lead, or not.

34

☆ To speed up your search for one of the jobs that *are* out there, *knock on doors* -- particularly if you *hate* to use the telephone.

Choose places where you would like to work. Either from the phone book, or by walking down those streets in your village, city, or town, where you would like to work. Then, physically go in there, at any place that looks interesting, and looks as though it might be hiring someone with your skills.

This tip, to state it in another way, is that if you want to speed up your job-hunt, you need to go *face-to-face* with employers whenever possible, rather than sending paper, such as a resume. 47.7% of those job-hunters who use this approach, get a hiring-interview and then a job, thereby.

Yes, I know this isn't easy, for most of us. But *if* nothing else is working, it's a good fall-back strategy for you to rely on.

Said one job-hunter: *"The very first real job I got was by knocking door-to-door, asking if they needed a draftsman. I got a favorable response at the fifth, but not the last, place I knocked; interviewed a few days after; and was working within the week. I was incredibly lucky, as were they: their current draftsman had given notice that day I knocked. I worked there two years and then went on to a much better position at the invitation of friends I had made at that first job."*

Generally speaking, and particularly at small organizations, it is the boss, or hiring manager -- the one who makes the actual decision to hire -- that you want to talk to, to ask if they're hiring.

When you knock on the doors of larger organizations, you will generally be well-advised to try to avoid the personnel or human resources department, since their primary function is often to *screen out* job-hunters, so as not to bother the people 'upstairs' -- though there are exceptions to this rule, where the department is helpful, kind, and capable of hiring. It's a judgment call, on your part. *(You are only likely to run into such departments if you are knocking on the door of larger organizations, inasmuch as only 15% of all organizations, mostly large ones, even have such departments.)*

Coming in 'cold' this way, if the only person you can manage to see is the receptionist or human resources department, they will ask you to fill out a job application.

Job applications are question-and-answer forms which have such simple questions as: Your Name, Address, Age, Places of Previous Employment. etc. Such applications vary greatly in their complexity, from ones used by fast-food chains, to those used by, say, engineering firms. *If* you decide to fill one out, use a black pen, *print* neatly, fill in every question or space, even questions that don't apply to you (write *n.a.* "not applicable" in that space), write *"Open"* for salary, and sign your name. If they ask your reasons for leaving a previous job, you can choose between: *the job ended, my family needed me at the time (no longer a problem), it was a seasonal job, it was a temporary job, I wanted to make a career change, I want more responsibility than they gave me.* (Courtesy of Dean Curtis.)

If you've never seen a job application in your life, and you plan to be approaching organizations *cold*, you should familiarize yourself with an application form ahead of time. One way to do this without jeopardizing your job chances at places you care about, is to go to visit some fast-food place or any large organization that has a personnel department where you *don't* care to work, and simply *ask* for a job application, then immediately go back out the door. Take the application form home with you, where you can study it, and take a stab at filling it out, just for practice. Then throw it in the waste basket, after you've learned what you need to know. Do *not* return it to the place you got it from, unless you are seriously interested in working there. The purpose of this exercise is simply to find out what an application form looks like, not to use it -- at least at this point. Anyway, now you know what an application form looks like, and how to fill it out. I hope you never need to.

This direct 'walk-in' approach may pay off for you, or it may not. The effectiveness of the approach to employers is probably in inverse proportion to the level sought: more effective for blue-collar jobs than for managerial ones. In their pioneering study of the job-hunt some years ago, *The Job Hunt: Job-Seeking Behavior of Unemployed Workers in a Local Economy,* Harvey Belitsky and Harold A. Sheppard discovered that going face-to-face at a workplace, without introduction or *leads,* was *the* most effective job-hunting method *if you were a blue-collar worker.* Blue-collar workers take note.

35

☆ To speed up your search for one of the jobs that *are* out there, be willing to look at different *kinds* of jobs: full-time jobs, part-time jobs, unlimited contract jobs *(formerly called 'permanent jobs'),* short-term contract jobs, temporary jobs, working for others, working for yourself, etc.

36

☆ To speed up your search for one of the jobs that *are* out there, always remember that no matter what handicaps you bring with you to the job-hunt, there are **two** kinds of employers out there: *those who will be put off by your handicap, and therefore won't hire you;*

AND

those who will not be put off by your handicap, and therefore will hire you, if you are qualified for the job.

You are not interested in the former kind of employer, no matter how many of them there are -- except as a source of referrals.

You are only looking for those employers who are not put off by your handicap, and therefore will hire you *if you can do the job.*

Once you get an invitation to come in for a hiring-interview with the-person-who-has-the-power-to-hire, you will of course want some tips about how to conduct the interview. Even at the interview stage, things can drag on and on. You want to do more than simply get interviews; you want them to result in your getting hired. Hence, the need for tips about how to conduct the interview successfully. Here they are:

37

☆ To increase your chances of getting hired early on, if it is you who is asking for the interview with the boss, only ask for twenty minutes; and keep to this, religiously. Don't stay *one minute longer!* This will always impress an employer!

38

☆ To increase your chances of getting hired early on, research the organization ahead of time, before going in for an interview. This will put you ahead (in the employer's mind) of the other people they talk to.

Toward this end, when the appointment is first set up, ask them right then and there if they have anything *in writing* about their organization; if so, request they mail it to you, so you'll have time to read it before the interview. Or, if the interview is the next day, offer to come down today and pick it up, yourself.

Also, go to your local library, and ask the librarian for help in locating any newspaper articles or other information about that organization.

Finally, ask all your friends if they know anyone who is working there, or used to work there; if they do, ask them to put you in touch with him or her, *please*.

You want to become familiar with the organization's history, their purposes and their goals. All organizations, be they large or small, profit or nonprofit, love to be loved. If you have gone to all this trouble, to learn so much about them -- before you ever walk in their doors, they will be impressed, believe me, because most job-hunters never go to this trouble. *They* walk in knowing little or nothing about the organization. This drives employers *nuts*. Want some examples?

One time, the first question an IBM college recruiter asked a graduating senior was, "What do the initials IBM stand for?" The senior didn't know, and the interview was over.

Another time, an employer said to me, "I'm so tired of job-hunters who come in, and say, *"Uh, what do you do here?"* that the next time someone walks in who already knows something about us, I'm going to hire him or her, on the spot." And he did, within the week.

Thus, if *you* come in, and have done your homework on the organization, this immediately makes you stand out from other job-hunters, and dramatically speeds up your chances of being offered a job there.

39

☆ To increase your chances of getting hired early on, do not hog the whole interview. Studies have revealed that generally speaking the people who get hired are those who mix speaking and listening fifty-fifty in the interview. That is, half the time they spend letting the employer do the talking, half the time in the interview the job-hunter does the talking. People who didn't follow that mix, were the ones who didn't get hired, according to the study.[9] My hunch as to the *reason* why this is so, is that if you talk too much about yourself, you come across as one who would ignore the needs of the organization; while if you talk too little, you come across as trying to hide something about your background.

40

☆ To increase your chances of getting hired early on, studies[10] have revealed that when it is your turn to speak, you should not speak any longer than two minutes at a time, if you want to make the best impression. In fact, a good answer to an employer's question sometimes only takes twenty seconds to give. This is useful information for you to know, in conducting a successful interview -- as you certainly want to do.

9. This one done by a researcher at Massachusetts Institute of Technology.

10. This one conducted by my colleague, Daniel Porot, in Geneva, Switzerland.

41

☆ To increase your chances of getting hired early on, stay focussed on what you can do for the employer, rather than on what the employer can do for you. You want the employer to see you as a potential *Resource Person* for that organization, rather than as simply *A Job Beggar* (to quote Daniel Porot). You want to come across as *a problem solver*, rather than as *one who simply keeps busy.*

42

☆ To increase your chances of getting hired early on, think of what a *bad* employee would do, in the position you are asking for -- come in late, take too much time off, follow his or her own agenda instead of the employer's, etc. Then emphasize to the employer how much you are the very opposite: your sole goal is to increase the organization's effectiveness and service and bottom line.

Every organization has two main preoccupations for its day-by-day work: the problems they are facing, and what solutions people are coming up with, there. Therefore, the main thing the employer is trying to figure out during the hiring-interview, is -- if they hire you -- will you be part of the *solution* there, or just another part of the *problem.*

During the course of the interview, you need to make it clear that you are there in order to make an oral proposal, followed hopefully by a written proposal, of what *you can do for them*, to help them with *their* problems. You will see immediately what a switch this is from the way most job-hunters approach an employer! *("How much do you pay, and how much time off will I have?")* Will he or she be glad to see you, with this different emphasis? In most cases, you bet they will. They *want* a resource person, and a problem-solver.

They are also looking for employees: *who are punctual, arriving at work on time or early; who stay until quitting time, or even leave late; who are dependable; who have a good attitude; who have drive, energy, and enthusiasm; who want more than a paycheck; who are self-disciplined, well-organized, highly motivated, and good at managing their time; who can handle people well; who can use language effectively; who can work on a computer; who are committed to team work; who are flexible, and can respond to novel situations, or adapt when circumstances at work change; who are trainable, and love to learn; who are project-oriented, and goal-oriented; who have creativity and are good at problem solving; who have integrity; who are loyal to the organization; who are able to identify opportunities, markets, coming trends. They also want to hire people who can bring in more money than they are paid.* Claim any of these that you *legitimately* can, during the hiring interview.

43

☆ To increase your chances of getting hired early on, be sure that you illustrate in the interview whatever it is you claim will be true of you, once hired. For example, if you claim you are very *thorough* in all your work, be sure to be thorough in the way you have researched the organization ahead of time. Overall, remember that the manner in which you do your job-hunt and the manner in which you would do the job you are seeking, are not assumed by most employers to be two unrelated subjects, but one and the same. They can tell when you are doing a slipshod, half-hearted job-hunt (*"Uh, what do you guys do here?"*) and this is taken as a clear warning that you might do a slipshod, half-hearted job, were they foolish enough to ever hire you. Employers know this simple truth: most people job-hunt the way they live their lives.

44

☆ To increase your chances of getting hired early on, try to think of some way to bring evidence of your skills. For example, if you are an artist, craftsperson or anyone who produces a product, try to bring a sample of what you have made or produced -- either in person, or through photos, or even videotapes.

As you will see from the diagram on the next page, employers have their own *hierarchy* of the ways in which they prefer to hire. Their most preferred method is at the bottom of the pyramid. Their least preferred method is at the apex.

The words within the triangle illustrate the typical employer's thoughts.

As you can see, the employer most prefers to hire from within, or to hire someone whose work he or she has seen. By bringing this evidence, this sort of *portfolio*, you are following the employer's preferred strategy: "I want to hire someone whose work I have seen."

Incidentally, while you are looking at this diagram, notice that the typical job-hunter hunts for a job *in exactly the opposite order* from the order that most employers prefer. This is why I call the job-hunting system in this country and most others, Neanderthal.

The way a typical job-hunter likes to hunt for a job (starts here)

6 "I will place an ad to find someone."
Newspaper Ads

Resumes
5 "I will look at some resumes which come in, unsolicited."

Employment Agency for Lower Level Jobs
"I want to hire someone for a lower level job, from a stack of potential candidates that some agency has screened **4** for me."

This is called 'a private employment agency,' or - - if it is within the company - - 'the human resources department,' formerly the 'personnel department.' Incidentally, only 15% of all organizations have such an internal department.

Search Firm for Higher Level Jobs
"I want to hire someone for a higher level job, from among outstanding people who are presently working **3** for another organization; and I will pay a recruiter to find this outstanding candidate for me."

The agency, thus hired by an employer, is called 'a search firm' or 'headhunter'; only employers can hire such agencies.

A Job-Hunter Who Offers Proof
"I want to hire someone who walks in the door and can show me samples of their previous work."
2 "I want to hire someone whose work a trusted friend of mine has seen and recommends."

That friend may be: mate, best friend, colleague in the same field, or colleague in a different field.

From Within
Employer's Thoughts:
1 "I want to hire someone whose work I have seen." (Promotion from within of a full-time employee, or promotion from within of a part-time employee; hiring a former consultant for a regular position (formerly on a limited contract); hiring a temp for a regular position; hiring a volunteer for a regular position.)

The way a typical employer prefers to fill vacancies (starts here)

Our Neanderthal Job-Hunting System

45

☆ To increase your chances of getting hired early on, never speak badly of your previous employer(s). Employers often feel as though they are a fraternity or sorority. During the interview you want to come across as one who displays courtesy toward all members of that fraternity or sorority. Bad-mouthing a previous employer only makes this employer worry that were they to hire you, you would end up bad-mouthing *them.*

I once spoke graciously about a previous employer, to my present employer. Unbeknownst to me, my present employer *knew* my previous employer had badly mistreated me. He therefore thought very highly of me because I didn't drag it up. In fact, he never forgot this incident; talked about it for years, afterward. It always makes a *big* impression when you don't bad-mouth a previous employer.

Say something nice about your previous employer, or if you know the previous employer is going to give you a very bad recommendation, just say something simple like, "I usually get along with everybody; but for some reason, my past employer and I just didn't get along. Don't know why. It's never happened to me before. Hope it never happens again."

46

☆ To increase your chances of getting hired early on, don't be wearied by rejection. Tom Jackson's model (from *Guerrilla Tactics in the Job Market*) of the typical job-hunt is:
NO NO NO NO NO NO NO NO NO NO NO NO NO NO
NO NO NO NO NO NO NO NO NO NO NO NO NO NO
NO NO NO NO NO NO NO NO NO NO NO NO NO NO
NO NO NO NO NO NO NO NO NO NO NO NO NO NO
NO NO NO NO NO NO NO NO NO NO NO NO NO NO
NO NO NO NO NO NO NO NO NO NO NO NO NO YES.[11]

---

11. This is my friend Tom Jackson's description of the typical job-hunt, in his famous book, *Guerrilla Tactics in the Job Market.*

Even in consecutive interviews at many places, the more NOs you get out of the way, the closer you are to YES. Ideally, of course, you want to end up with two YESes. Two, so that you'll have at least two things to choose between.

47

☆ To increase your chances of getting hired early on, every evening after an interview sit down and write (with pen, typewriter, keyboard/printer), or e-mail, a thank-you note to each person you saw that day. This means not only employers, but also their secretaries, receptionists, or anyone else who gave you a friendly helping hand, in any way. Don't make this *perfunctory*. Make it personal. Mention something individual about the way they treated you, or what you liked about them. Use the thank-you note to underline anything that was discussed during the interview, or to add anything you left out, that was important.

The thank-you note is *crucial*. A job-hunter presented herself for a hiring-interview as public relations officer for a major-league baseball team. That evening, she wrote and mailed a thank-you note. She was eventually hired for the job, and when she asked why, they told her that they had decided to hire her because, out of thirty-five applicants, she was the only one who had written a thank-you note after the interview.

If you want to stand out from the others applying for the same job, if you want to speed up your getting hired, send thank-you notes -- to *everyone* you met there, that day.

Treat every employer with courtesy, even if it seems certain they can offer you no job there; they may be able to refer you to someone else next week, if you made a good impression.

WHAT IF NOTHING WORKS?

Following the strategies in this chapter, learned from *successful* job-hunters, you should dramatically improve your chance of finding a job.[12] Good luck, and if you find one, congratulations. You do not need to read the rest of this book -- *until the next time.*

But if you faithfully try everything listed in this chapter, and *none of it works* for you, what then? Well, there is a life-preserver still available to you: flee to Chapters 5, 6, and 7. read them, and painstakingly do the exercises in *The Parachute Workbook* (it will take you no more than a good weekend, if you keep at it).

Above all, never abandon hope, my friend.

I close this chapter, with the story of a successful job-hunter, who wrote me as follows:

"I was a woman who majored in Humanities and then floated around after college in several jobs, which were just jobs. To be honest, I was in my early twenties (which I have nicknamed the decade of terror), and had no idea what I wanted to do. Only, I longed for self-expression and passion in my work. I purchased your book, did some informational interviews, even saw a career counselor, all to no avail.

"Five years later, now, I have come back to your book (the new edition, of course), and identified my values, skills and talents. With my values and skills in mind, I went to the library to research government and non-profit careers, and found myself much interested in the latter. I copied a list of them and began contacting the organizations whose values were closely related to mine: helping people in the community.

---

12. If you want more job-hunting strategies, I refer you to *The Complete Job and Career Handbook: 101 Ways to Get From Here to There,* by S. Norman Feingold and Marilyn N. Feingold. Garrett Park Press, PO Box 190B, Garrett Park, MD 20896. 1993. This $15 book lists many other strategies for you to explore, should your job-hunt reach a dead end. Chapter titles include: "Infrequently Used/Non-traditional Job and Career Search Techniques," "Check List of 177 Ways to Help Get A Job and Advance Your Career," etc. Very helpful, and detailed. Dr. Feingold is a pioneer in the career counseling field, and he and Marilyn really know their stuff.

"One organization in particular called me back the next day, and asked if I could interview for a professional position with them. I did, explored further to be sure I understood what the job entailed, interviewed a second time, and in less than one month was offered the position of my dreams!

"Thanks to you and your advice on the most successful ways to find employment -- previously, over a period of four months, I had applied for at least fifty jobs from the want ads, with no hits -- I am now happily employed doing the kind of work I like best, and I did so in record time."

*To grow is to change, and to become perfect
is to change often.*

Cardinal Newman

FOR THE IMPATIENT JOB-HUNTER

HOW TO QUICKLY CHOOSE A NEW CAREER

WHEN YOU HAVEN'T THE FOGGIEST IDEA WHAT YOU WANT TO DO

Chapter 4

Table of Contents

HOW DO PEOPLE CHOOSE CAREERS?

Once, I overheard two college students talking, in Central Park in New York City. We'll call them Jim and Fred. In half a minute of conversation they perfectly illustrated the way most people choose careers:

Jim: Hey, what are you majoring in?

Fred: Physics.

Jim: Physics? Man, you shouldn't major in physics.
    Computer science is the thing these days.

Fred: Naw, I like physics.

Jim: Man, physics doesn't pay much.

Fred: Really? What does?

Jim: Computer science. You should switch to computer science.

Fred: Okay, I'll look into it tomorrow.

In this way are many career choices (and career-changes) made in our culture -- on impulse and whim, in a moment, in the twinkling of an eye. A casual conversation with someone. A decision to just follow in our parents' footsteps. An article on a news broadcast. An invitation from a girlfriend or boyfriend to come work where they do.

> When you choose a career,[1] you have got to know what it is you *want* to do, or else someone is going to sell you a bill of goods somewhere along the line that can do irreparable damage to your self-esteem, your sense of worth, and your stewardship of the talents that God gave you.

Most of us spend more time planning next summer's vacation, which will consume about 80 hours of our life, than we spend planning our life in the world of work, which will consume 80,000 hours of our life.

You'd think we'd spend some time trying to figure out what we want to do with our lives. Instead, we take shortcuts in deciding on a career. And most of those shortcuts begin not by

---

1. The word **career** remains a very fuzzy word in the English language, because there are three senses in which it is used. It is used, first of all, to mean *work* in contrast to *learning* or *leisure*. Thus when clothing ads speak of "a career outfit," they are referring to clothes which are worn primarily at work, rather than during learning-activities or leisure-activities. It is used, secondly, to sum up *a person's whole life in the world of work*. Thus when people say of someone at the end of their life, "He or she had a brilliant career," they are not referring to a particular occupation, but to *all* the occupations this person ever held, and all the work this person ever did. Thirdly, in its most common sense, as I indicated earlier, it is used as a synonym for the word *occupation* or *job* -- particularly where that occupation or job offers opportunity for promotion and advancement, toward the top. (This *movement toward a goal* is its most primitive meaning, as it dates from the origin of the word. *Career* comes from the Latin *carrus*, referring to a racetrack where horses wildly *careen* while competing in a race.) The wild way in which people *careen* into careers thus preserves the original meaning of the word. *Adapted from the article on "Careers" in* Collier's Encyclopedia, *written by the author. Copyright © 1991 by Macmillan Educational Company.*

inquiring what *we* want to do, but by trying to figure out what *the job-market* supposedly is looking for.

U.S. Statistics

A survey found that 45% of all U.S. workers said they would change their careers if they could.[2]

In point of fact, each year about 10% of all U.S. workers actually do. In the most recent year surveyed, that equated to 10 million workers who changed careers that year. Of these:

5.3 million of them changed careers *voluntarily*, and in 7 out of 10 cases their income went up;

1.3 million of them changed careers *involuntarily*, because of what happened to them in the economy, and in 7 out of 10 cases, their income went down;

3.4 million of them changed careers for a *mixture* of voluntary and involuntary reasons (such as needing to go from part-time to full-time work, etc.), and there is no record of what happened to their income.

Despite the *myth* that career-change is primarily a mid-life phenomenon, in point of fact people can and do change careers at *all* ages. In this study, only one out of ten career-changers was actually in mid-life.[3] Many U.S. experts think, however, that the remainder of the '90s will see a lot more 'mid-life career-change,' inasmuch as 1996 was the year when the first of the U.S.'s 76 million 'baby boomers' turned fifty. The rest are only in their forties, at best.

---

2. The survey was done for by by the Roper Organization for Shearson Lehman Brothers, in 1992.

3. The year was 1986. The survey was published in the *Occupational Outlook Quarterly,* Summer 1989, and in the *Monthly Labor Review,* September 1989. Should you wish further resources dealing with career-change at mid-life, these include:

Betsy Jaffe, Ed.D., *Altered Ambitions: What's Next in Your Life? Winning Strategies To Reshape Your Career.* Donald I. Fine, Inc., 19 W. 21st St., New York, NY 10010. 1991.

Godfrey Golzen, and Philip Plumbley, *Changing Your Job After 35.* Kogan Page Ltd., 120 Pentonville Rd., London N1 9JN. 1988.

Tell me, we say, *what kinds of careers are doing a lot of hiring, these days?* Or, *Tell me,* we say, *what are the careers where I can make the most money?* Or, *Tell me,* we say, *what are the hot careers for the next ten years?* The answers we get, from so-called experts, are often far wide of the mark! *Beware of false prophets,* someone once said. Good advice, when trying to guess 'the best future careers.' We read about these supposedly great jobs, we go looking for one, and often we cannot find it no matter how hard we look. One year, two years, still can't find one.

But even when we do, it turns out there's often a chasm the size of the Grand Canyon between what we thought we were going to be doing vs. what we actually wind up doing. For example, we thought we were going to be working with people all day long, helping, caring, but we discover -- too late -- that most of the day we're only working with paper. Or we thought we were going to be working on the computer designing gorgeous images, and we discover -- too late -- that most of the day is spent in meetings. We start reading *Dilbert* avidly. *The vision vs. the reality.* What a letdown!

No wonder surveys of worker dissatisfaction find that up to 80%, or four out of every five workers, are dissatisfied with some important aspects of their jobs or careers. *It's not a pretty picture.*

Used by permission of Johnny Hart and Creators Syndicate, Inc.

WHAT PUSHES US TO
CHANGE CAREERS?

It is no surprise that as time goes on, we decide to change careers. Not once, but several times in our life. In fact, people entering the job-market today should count on having anywhere between three and six careers during their lifetime.

We make this decision to change careers for one of several reasons:

• We got fired, and we can't find our old work any more; we *have* to 're-tool.'

• We are not earning enough, and we need a new career that pays us more money -- more of what we're worth.

• We made a bad choice when we first chose our career, and now we've decided to set it right.

• All we wanted from a job, in the past, was money; now we want *meaning*. Indeed, if truth be told, most of us are engaged in a life-long search for, and journey toward, *meaning* -- a process in which career-choice plays an important part.

• We're looking more and more for 'our mission in life,' and while we don't yet know what that is, we do know for sure that what we're presently doing *isn't it*.

• We've been asked to do the work of three, and we feel stressed out, angry, exhausted, burnt out, and grumpy; we want a job or career that is a little easier on us, so we'll have time to smell the flowers.

• We had hardly been stretched at all by our previous work, and we'd like something that offers a real challenge and 'stretches' us.

• We had a dream job, but our much-beloved boss moved on, we now find ourselves working for 'a jerk,' and the dream job has turned into 'the job from hell.' We not only want a new employer, we want a new career.

For any or all of these reasons, we change careers.

SELF-EMPLOYMENT

Sometimes the career we change to is that of self-employment. 12% of all the workers in the U.S. are self-employed. But of course, that means that 88% of all the workers in the U.S. are working for someone else.

In view of this disparity, I have put notes, about self-employment, in the *Workbook*, on page *85*, for the 12% *(one would guess)* of my readers who are interested in that possibility; but am devoting the remainder of this chapter to the vast majority (88%) whose idea of career-change is that of moving to a new career, but still working for someone else.

I would, however, caution those leaning toward self-employment to read this chapter as well. For, self-employment is a career-change, for sure; and the better you understand what career-change is, the better your transition to self-employment may be.

WHAT CAREER-CHANGE IS

Okay, then, let's begin. Simply. Basically, a career is made up of two parts: an occupation-title, and a field. For example, let us suppose you decided you wanted to be a management consultant. That's an occupation-title. So far, so good. But, you have to go beyond that, and decide also on a field.

In what field do you want to be a management consultant? Do you want to do management consulting with . . . a law firm? . . . a gardening firm? . . . a camping firm? . . . a firm that manufactures cars? . . . a computer firm? . . . or what? Makes a big difference, doesn't it? Law, Gardening, Camping, Cars, Computers -- these are all *fields*.

Career-change = *occupation-title* + *field*. Memorize that, please. It will help you a lot, down the line. If you're trying hard to find a job as a management consultant, for example, and nothing is turning up, you know what your problem is. You only said, "I want to be a management consultant," and that by itself isn't enough. It's an occupation-title, to be sure. But, if you want your job-hunt to be successful you must also define a *field.* Until you've decided what field you want to do management consulting in, your job-hunt is going to be somewhere between *difficult* and *impossible.* Too broad a target, too dispersed, too scattered. You need to focus your job-hunt, or career-change. *Field* is the way you do that.

So, this is our first lesson: *Career-change = occupation-title + field.* And in the most complete career-change you move from one occupation-title to another, *and* from one field to another. Let me illustrate:

Types of Career Change Visualized

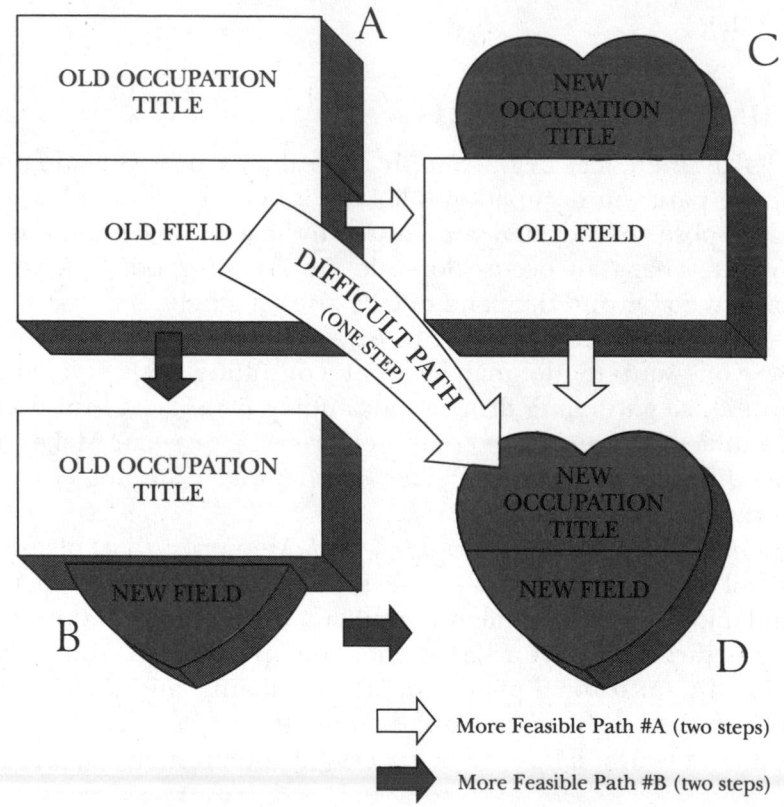

More Feasible Path #A (two steps)

More Feasible Path #B (two steps)

WHEN YOU KNOW WHAT
CAREER YOU WANT:
THE 'ONE STEP AT A TIME'
METHOD OF CHANGING
CAREERS

As the previous diagram makes clear, when you've decided it's time for you to make a career-change, there are three kinds of career change you can choose:

(1) You can just change your field but not your occupation-title. This is a move from A to B, in the diagram. *This is a career-change. You may be much happier just by getting into a new* field.

(2) You can just change your occupation-title, but not your field. This is a move from A to C, in the diagram. *This is a career-change. You may be much happier just by changing your* occupation, *in that same field.*

(3) You can decide you want to change both your occupation-title *and* your field. This is a move from A to D, in the diagram. *This is a career-change. You may decide you can only be happy if you change both* occupation *and* field.

Should you decide you want to make the latter kind of complete change, there are two ways you can go about it:

a) The move can be made all at once (The Difficult Path) -- going from A to D, in a single bound.

b) Or, the move can be made in two steps, as indicated by the two white arrows (that's one way), or by the two red arrows (that's another way). We call this the 'one-step-at-a-time' method of career change.

To illustrate all of this, let us suppose your present (or most recent) career is that of an accountant at a television station. Now, for whatever reason, you've decided that you would like to change careers, and be a reporter who covers the medical field.

If you decide to try to make this career-change in a single bound, you go and try to convince some newspaper, journal, or whatever that you have the expertise and background to be a good reporter, *and* that you also are familiar with the medical field. This is not easy -- unless you have some background

Types of Career Change Visualized

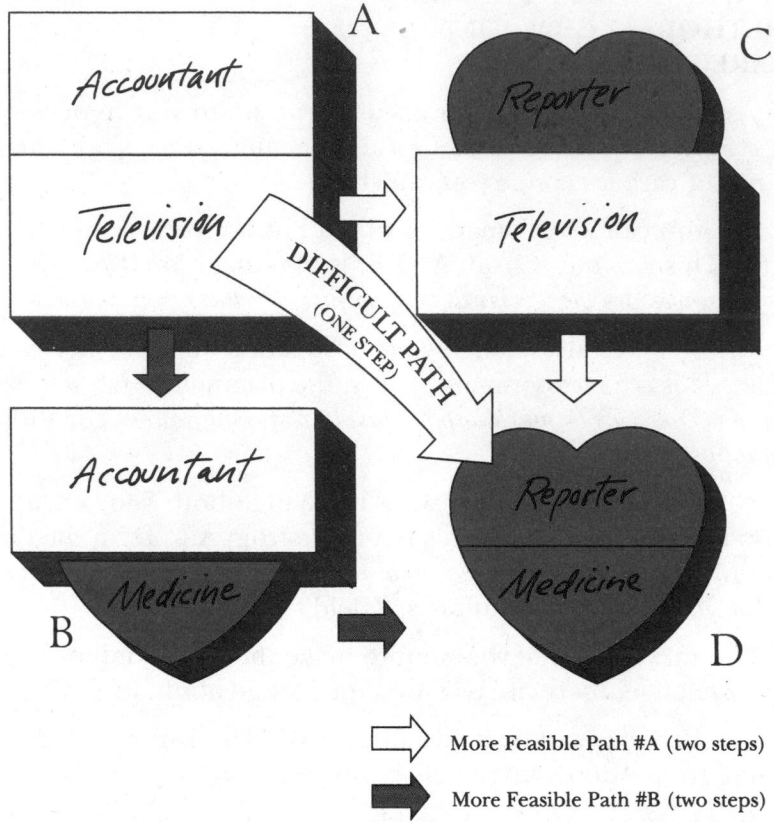

More Feasible Path #A (two steps)

More Feasible Path #B (two steps)

and experience in both -- and that's why we call this The Difficult Path. But there is another way -- two other ways, as a matter of fact.

In the diagram above, you can first move from A to B: stay an accountant, but get a new job at some medical journal or newspaper. You'd stay there one year, two, or three; then you move from B to D: try to get them to hire you as a reporter where you are, or try to get a different medical journal or newspaper to hire you as a reporter.

Alternatively, you can first move from A to C: ask the television station where you already work as an accountant to hire you as a reporter instead, or go to another television station and ask to be hired as a reporter. You'd stay there one year, two, or three; then you move from C to D: getting a job as a reporter at a medical journal or newspaper.

> In both cases, the tremendous advantage of this 'one-step-at-a-time' career-change method, is that *each time you make a move, you are already experienced in either the occupation or the field.* This carries much greater weight with would-be employers, than when you are inexperienced in both occupation *and* field at the same time.

SELLING YOURSELF
TO AN EMPLOYER
WHEN YOU ARE INEXPERIENCED

But suppose you've found the career of your dreams. You want to get there in a single bound. You don't want to take it in steps. How do you sell yourself to a would-be employer, when you are inexperienced in both occupation *and* field?

In such a case, you must remember that every occupation is composed of a series of tasks or assignments, and every task or assignment, in turn, requires that you have certain skills, to do it well.

You can quickly learn just exactly what skills are required for this new career of yours, by going and chatting with people who are already in that career. *What tasks or assignments do you have to do in this career?* you ask them. And, *What skills does it take to do such tasks or assignments?* Armed with such a list, after interviewing two or three, you can then compare it with the skills that *you* have, and put a check beside each skill that matches. After which, you can approach a would-be employer, for this new career you have chosen, as someone who is *experienced.* Of course you are brand new to both occupation and field, but you *are* experienced where it really counts. And that is, in your skills. Indeed, precisely those skills needed to do the tasks and assignments of this new job and career.

You can not only enumerate what those skills are, but you can give the employer convincing evidence and proof, from the past, that you have those skills.

True, you used them in a different occupation and field at the time. But all skills are *transferable*. That is, if you were good -- say -- at *analyzing things,* in the past, you will be good at *analyzing things* in this new occupation, and field. '*Analyzing things*' is not just a skill; it is a '*transferable* skill.'

If you did enough chatting with people in this new career of yours before you approach an employer, you will also have gained a considerable overview of the field and occupation -- even though you've never been in it -- and to that degree you will be *familiar* with both, in at least some small degree, as would not be the case if you had never done all that chatting.

It is obvious of course that before approaching an employer, you *will* have to do some homework on yourself. Specifically, you will need to take an inventory of just exactly what your transferable skills are.

That takes time. That takes patience. And it requires a systematic method.

Such a method is described in the next chapters, "For the Determined Job-Hunter," and in The Workbook that you will find in *The Parachute Workbook and Resource Guide,* attached to this book.

We can thus supply you with the method.

You have to supply the time. And the patience.

WHEN YOU DON'T KNOW
WHAT CAREER YOU WANT

When you have no idea what you'd like to do next, there is only one route that makes any sense, as we have already seen:

> Don't decide on your future, until you have first inventoried your past.

The purpose of choosing or changing a career is to find career satisfaction, or -- in a word -- happiness. More than that, it is to find a career you will *love*. Work that you can't wait to get up in the morning and go do. Work that you love so much, you can't believe you are being paid to do it -- since you'd be willing to do it for nothing.

Finding a career you can love depends on there being a match between what you love most to do, and what is available *out there*. For example, if some *hot* new career is available, but involves working with paper, while you love working with people, then that career is going to make you miserable, no matter how easy it may be to find a job there.

Hence, it doesn't matter that a career is *hot* or *easy* to get into. What matters is that you and the career should be happy with each other, nay, be in love with each other. There are few greater joys in life, than to find such a career.

As we can see from the diagram on the next page, finding such a career depends upon it matching the skills you love to use, plus your favorite subjects, the people you love to help or work with, the kind of place where you love to work, your goals and that place's goals, and a salary that satisfies your needs.

Chief among these are the skills you love to use, and your favorite subjects. While you may think you know what these are, in most cases your self-knowledge could use a little more work. A weekend would do. In a weekend, you can inventory your past sufficiently so that you have a good picture of the *kind* of work you would love to be doing. You can, of course, stretch the inventory over a number of weeks, maybe doing an

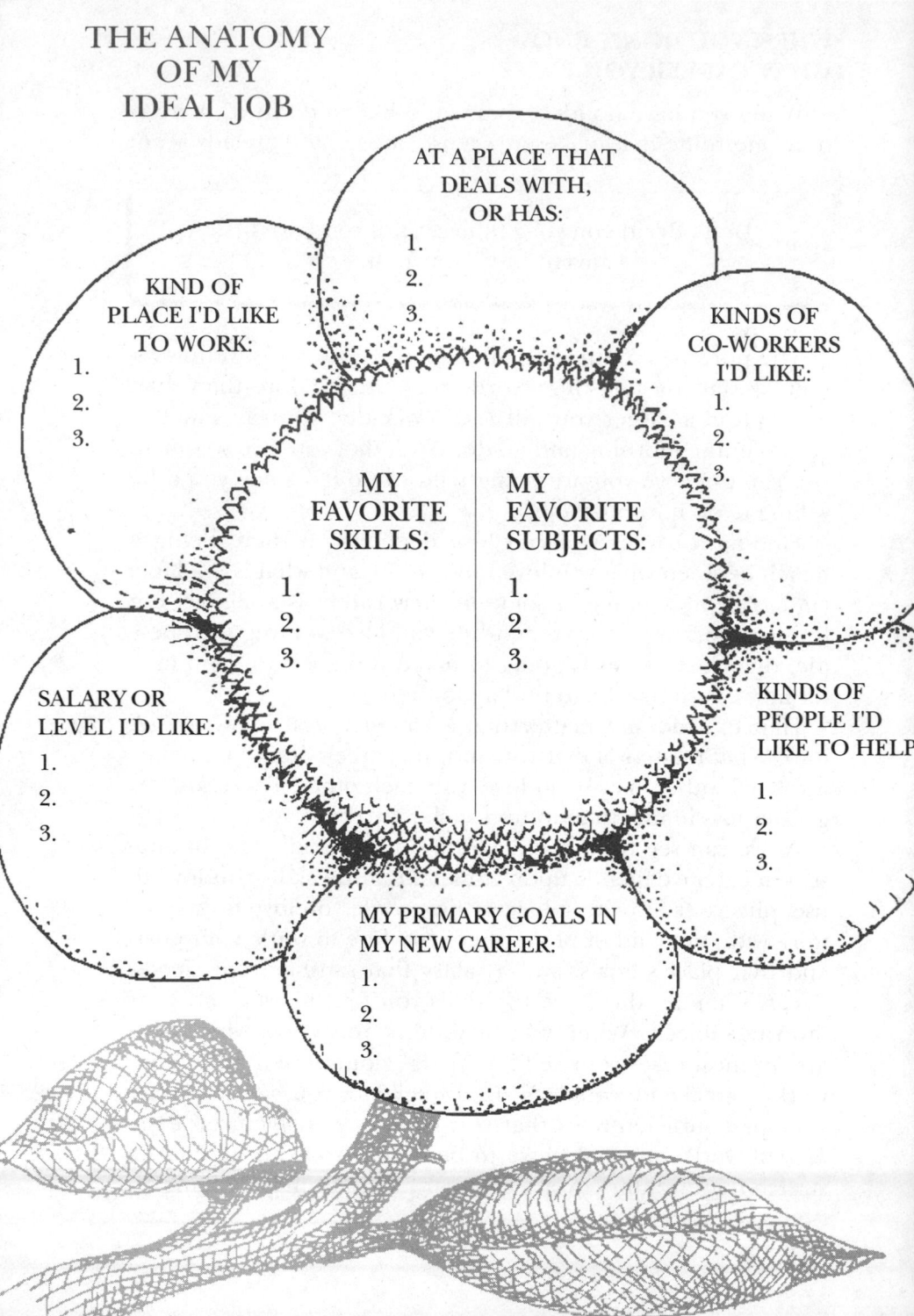

THE ANATOMY
OF MY
IDEAL JOB

AT A PLACE THAT
DEALS WITH,
OR HAS:
1.
2.
3.

KIND OF
PLACE I'D LIKE
TO WORK:
1.
2.
3.

KINDS OF
CO-WORKERS
I'D LIKE:
1.
2.
3.

MY
FAVORITE
SKILLS:
1.
2.
3.

MY
FAVORITE
SUBJECTS:
1.
2.
3.

SALARY OR
LEVEL I'D LIKE:
1.
2.
3.

KINDS OF
PEOPLE I'D
LIKE TO HELP:
1.
2.
3.

MY PRIMARY GOALS IN
MY NEW CAREER:
1.
2.
3.

hour or two one night a week, if you prefer. It's up to you as to just how you do it.

But it is the best way. Indeed, it is the only sensible path to career satisfaction. *Don't decide on your future before you have first inventoried your past.*

The Best Way to Choose A New Career

You do a systematic inventory of the *transferable skills* which you already possess, and the *bodies of knowledge* which you already know, together with *the interests* that most fascinate you, and from all this you fashion a description -- a picture, if you will -- of what your new career *looks like*, then you interview people, with this picture, to find out *what its name is* (or names). The inventory takes a weekend. The finding out of the names takes several hours of research during the weeks following.

A detailed description of this process of career-change is in *The Parachute Workbook and Resource Guide* attached to this book at the back. The workbook is called "The Quick Job-Hunting Map," subtitled, *How to Create A Picture of Your Ideal Job or Next Career.*

SHORTCUTS

Now, this careful, reasoned way of going about choosing or changing a career is by far the best way. But you may feel that you just don't have the time or the patience to do all this work of inventorying your past.

That, of course, is how you feel *now*. It may be, that in a few weeks or months, you will feel quite differently, in which case we'll see you back here. Keep it in mind as *Plan B*, if the other things you try just don't work out.

In the meantime, for the Patience-Impaired, we'll devote the remainder of this chapter to looking at some shortcuts.

Ah, shortcuts, you say. What a lovely word.

Yes, shortcuts. But do remember that though they save time, you purchase that savings at a cost. You gain something, you lose something: accuracy. There's always the danger of *out of the frying pan, into the fire,* when you choose your new career in haste.

MIRROR, MIRROR, ON THE WALL, WHO'S THE FAIREST ONE OF ALL?

Well anyway, you want to know the simplest, fastest, easiest way to pick a career, I'm sure. Here is the fastest:

The Mirror Method of Choosing A New Career

In this method you use other people as though they were mirrors to yourself. You look at everyone you know, everyone you've ever seen on TV, or read about, and you think to yourself, "Well, whose job would I most like to have, in all the world?" Make a second and third choice. Write what each of these three people does, on three sheets of paper. Underneath each, then, break down their job into its parts: what is it about the job that attracts you? List as many things as possible. Then look at all three sheets of paper, choose which job is actually of greatest interest to you, and figure out how you could get such a job.

One woman who changed careers this way decided that the job she most admired was that of a woman she saw on national TV, who hosted a children's program. So, she prepared a careful outline of what she thought a good children's TV program should look like, then went to her local TV station (which had no such program) and told them her ideas. They liked her proposal, hired her to host just such a program, and she became a big success. Later, she triumphantly wrote me, "I am in my ideal career. . . . without ever having done any of the exercises in your book!" *Bravo,* say I.

This assumes, of course, that you can move from one career into another without spending much time 're-tooling.'

NEXT: A VOCATIONAL RESTAURANT

Now to our second shortcut: *Lists.*

When it's time to choose or change careers, many of us would like to be able to sit down in some kind of Vocational Restaurant, and just choose from a menu of options.

Big problem: there is no such Restaurant, *and* the number of options is bewildering. For example, experts can name at least 12,860 different occupations or careers that you might choose from, and these have 8,000 alternative job-titles, for a total of over 20,000.[4]

Twenty thousand! There's the problem, right there. Most of us find it is impossible to choose between 20,000 of anything. In fact, we have trouble choosing between twenty items on a restaurant menu!

That's why our experts have hacked this list down, essentially, to just 300 options. Yes, you can find 90% of the 125 million workers in the U.S. in a mere 300 of those 20,000 job-titles. The other 19,700 job titles are filled by just 10% of the workforce.

Some experts have hacked the list down further still, to just 50 options. You can find 50% of the 125 million workers in the U.S. in just 50 job-titles.

---

4. A description of all 20,000 of these occupations or careers can be found in any U.S. library, in a volume known as the U.S. *Dictionary of Occupational Titles.* It is known more familiarly as the *D.O.T.*, and is published by the Bureau of Labor Statistics. Other countries sometimes have similar volumes.

The *D.O.T.* is updated periodically -- most recently in 1991, with the previous revision having occurred in 1977, and supplemented (only) in 1982, 1986, and 1987. While vocational experts always recommend using this directory, our readers have found it a *terribly unhelpful* book for the end of the twentieth century. As one reader, a chemist, wrote: "While it claims to be updated to 1991, I found that *every* description I looked up was last updated in 1977! [That's twenty years ago!] . . . I read the description of my present occupation and it sounds quite good. I only wish I was doing what it described. That may have been what a chemist did 20 years ago but with most companies de-emphasizing research it is hardly what they do today." If you want to dabble in the D.O.T. despite these warnings, be prepared for its description of a particular job or career to be *widely* divergent from what that job is, currently. Be sure to go talk to people actually doing what you'd like to do. They'll tell you what the job or career is really like, *now.*

Fifty would seem to be a manageable number of careers to choose between, but in our culture we're always looking for someone who will hack the list down, further still -- say, to just ten options. That's why so many magazines, books, and newspapers, publish such lists as *The Ten Hottest Fields of the '90s.*

Anything so that we don't have to work our way through twenty thousand choices!

LISTS OF 'GUESSES'

The 'Look Over This List' Method
of Choosing A New Career

In this method you look over a list of careers, or occupations, and see if any of them appeals to you. This approach assumes, of course, that you have at least a vague idea of what work these people do. If you don't know what 'a carpenter' does, then obviously you're not going to pick 'carpenter.' But, anyway, let's try it and see how it goes, for you.

We'll start with the shortest lists. They always have just ten items on them, and are usually titled "The Top Ten" something or other. They are *interesting*, sometimes helpful, sometimes useless. The most useless are lists of 'the ten *hottest* occupations.' (Whatever *that* means.)

• List #1. A Typical List of Someone's Idea of 'The Ten Best Careers':

> *Computer animator*, Online content producer, *Mutual fund manager*, Industrial environmentalist, *Family doctor*, Management consultant, *Intellectual property lawyer*, Priest, rabbi, minister, *Interactive ad executive*, and Physical therapist.[5]

---

5. Or so *P.O.V.* Magazine says (quoted in *USA Today*, April 11, 1996).

How useful is such a list as this? Well, all such lists are highly subjective, they will differ from one magazine or book to another, there is no agreement between them all on which are really the 'ten hottest' careers, nor will they tell you what criteria they used when compiling that list.

That's for starters. More importantly, one person's *best career* is another person's *poison*. As you will recall, the best career *for You* has to: use *Your* favorite skills, *Your* favorite subjects, *Your* primary goals, and offer *Your* preferred people and things to work with, *Your* preferred workplace, that deals with *Your* preferred objectives, and all of this at *Your* preferred level and salary.

Thus it is, that each individual must form his or her *own* list of 'ten best careers.' (*See* The Workbook in *The Parachute Workbook and Resource Guide* attached to this book at the back.)

No one else can do this for you; therefore no one else's list should be taken seriously by you for even one minute -- unless you see something on that list that causes you to go, *Aha!*, triumphantly. It's given you an idea!

As a *primer of the pump*, such a list may be useful. As *a recipe* for where you should go next, it can be a disaster.

Next list?

Well actually, we have three -- all attempting to *predict* the labor market for the next decade:

- List #2. The top ten *occupations* that experts predict will grow the fastest between now and the year 2005:

    Personal and home care aides, Home health aides, *Systems analysts,* Computer engineers, *Physical and corrective therapy assistants and aides,* Electronic pagination systems workers, *Occupational therapy assistants and aides,* Physical therapists, *Residential counselors,* and Human services workers.[6]

- List #3. The top ten *occupations* ranked by the number of additional workers that experts predict will be needed by the year 2005 are:

    Cashiers, Janitors and cleaners, including maids and housekeeping cleaners, *Salespersons in retail,* Waiters and waitresses, *Registered nurses,* General managers and top executives, *Systems analysts,* Home health aides, *Guards,* and Nursing aides, orderlies and attendants.[7]

- List #4. The top ten *fields* that experts predict will grow the fastest between now and the year 2005:

    Health services (they think *this will grow 120% between 1995 and 2005),* Residential care (83%), *Business services (79%),* Automobile services (except repair) (75%), *Computer and data processing services (70%),* Individual and other social services (69%), *Health practitioners not described elsewhere (65%),* Child daycare services (59%), *Personnel supply services (58%),* Services to buildings (58%), *Equipment rental and leasing (51%),* and Securities sales and services (50%).[8]

Please note: none of these three lists are lists of *facts.* They are all lists of *guesses.* This is what labor market experts *guess* will happen between now and the year 2005. And you know how reliable *guesses* or *predictions* are. Read any weather reports lately?

---

6. The *Bureau of Labor Statistics,* December 1, 1995.

7. Ditto.

8. Ditto.

LISTS OF FACTS

If you want facts instead of guesses, here are five such lists. They all describe what is actually the case, right now, rather than what someone *guesses* will be the case by the year 2005.

• List #5. The fifty occupations that over half of the U.S. workforce are *actually* in, right now:

Automobile mechanics, carpenters, *electricians*, light- or heavy-truck drivers, *construction laborers*, welders & cutters, *groundskeepers & gardeners*, electrical and electronic engineers, *freight, stock, and material movers or handlers*, guards and police, *production occupations*, supervisors, *farmers*, commodities sales representatives, *laborers*, lawyers, *farm workers*, stockhandlers & baggers, *insurance sales*, janitors & cleaners, *managers & administrators*, supervisors & proprietors, *machine operators*, teachers -- university, college, secondary and elementary school, *stock & inventory clerks*, accountants & auditors, *underwriters and other financial officers*, secretaries, *receptionists*, childcare workers, *registered nurses*, typists, *bookkeepers*, textile sewing machine operators, *nursing aides*, orderlies & attendants, *hairdressers & cosmetologists*, waiters & waitresses, *maids and housemen*, cashiers, *general office clerks*, administrative support occupations, *sales workers*, computer operators, *miscellaneous food preparation occupations*, production inspectors, *checkers & examiners*, cooks, *real estate salespeople*, and assemblers.

• List #6. The ten U.S. occupations that are considered the most prestigious (in case you're hunting for respect):

Physician (Prestige Score: 82), *College professor (78)*, Judge (76), *Attorney (76)*, Astronomer (74), *Dentist (74)*, Bank officer (72), *Engineer (71)*, Architect (71), and *Clergy (70)*.[9]

• List #7. The ten U.S. *occupations* that actually pay the most, right now (just *in case* this is of any interest to you):

Physicians (Median salary: $148,000), *Dentists ($93,000)*, Lobbyists ($91,000), *Veterinarians ($63,069)*, Management

---

9. Source: The National Opinion Research Center.

consultants ($61,900), *Lawyers ($60,500)*, Electrical engineers ($59,100), *School principals ($57,300)*, Aeronautical engineers ($56,700), *Airline pilots ($56,500)*, and Civil engineers ($55,800).[10]

• List #8. The ten U.S. *fields* that actually pay the most, right now (we're talking 'median earnings' again):

Engineering, *mathematics*, computer and information sciences, *pharmacy*, architecture/environmental design, *physics*, accounting, *economics*, health/medical technologies, *and physical therapy*.[11]

• List #9. And finally, one extra list at no extra charge: the ten U.S. States with the lowest unemployment rate currently (just *in case* you are thinking about moving to where they're desperate for workers):

Nebraska (the lowest unemployment rate in the nation: only 2.39%), South Dakota (2.82%), *North Dakota (3.14%)*, Iowa (3.28%), *Utah (3.36%)*, Minnesota (3.45%), *Wisconsin (3.67%)*, Colorado (3.84 %), *New Hampshire (3.89%)*, and Delaware (4.11%).[12]

TRY ON THAT DRESS OR SUIT, FIRST, BEFORE YOU BUY

Now, let us suppose there is some career on the previous lists that sounds really intriguing to you. What should you do? Go get trained, get a degree (if that's necessary), and then go looking for jobs in the career you have chosen? No, no, no.

Before you take one single step toward pursuing that career, you *must* go talk to people in that career and see what it's *really* like -- lest you make a huge mistake.

Beyond chatting with them, you should, if the job lends itself to it,[13] ask if you can follow one of them around all day, to

10. Source: *Money* Magazine, and *The Bureau of Labor Statistics.*

11. Source: "Earnings of college graduates, 1993: Fields of study is a major determinant of the wide variations in earnings." *Monthly Labor Review,* December 1995.

12. *The Bureau of Labor Statistics.*

13. Well, I can think of some careers that don't: following a pilot around on his plane is one that comes to mind, and sitting in on a psychiatrist's sessions is another.

*"Let's put it this way — if you can find a village without
an idiot, you've got yourself a job."*

see what the job actually involves on an hour by hour basis.
Don't overlook this step. It is crucial, if you are to avoid being
miserable in your new career.

Let's say you're thinking about a new career where you
would be working in a beauty salon. You take the Yellow Pages,
look up the ones in your city or neighborhood, go down there
and ask to talk with someone who does the work you are thinking about doing. If you're still interested in the work, you then
talk to them (and their manager), tell them you're thinking
about going into this kind of work, and would it be possible
for you to volunteer to help out there for a day, and follow
someone around to see what the job actually involves? If they
say No, for any reason, go visit another salon, and make the
same request, until someone says, "Sure!"

You *need* to do this 'all-day visit,' because many jobs that
look interesting and glamorous at a distance, don't look so
glamorous up close. Standing on your feet all day, doing boring idle chit-chat, smelling awful odors, handling endless com-
plaints -- well, you get the picture. If all of this strikes you,

instead, as: painless exercise, good conversation, *interesting* odors, and challenges to be met and overcome, well then, you were probably born to do this work.

But that's exactly what you're trying to find out, one way or another. And you want to find it out, regardless of what career looks interesting on the list above. Before you go get trained to do it, you want to *try it on* first, even as you would a dress or suit before you buy. You want to understand the job fully and see what it feels like, from the inside, before you decide to commit.

Don't choose a career just because some expert says, *This is it!* Choose it because you love it, and you have taken the time to test that by 'on-the-job *shadowing*,' as I just described.

Otherwise, 'worker dissatisfaction' will soon be your favorite subject, and you're gonna be going through all this again, *real soon.*

GETTING A JOB BY DEGREES

But if you've explored this new career, and it still sounds interesting to you, then you can feel more confident you've made a good choice.

There is, however, another series of questions you *must* ask of those who are doing the work you are thinking about going into:

How do I get into this career, and how much of a demand is there for people who can do this work?

And, is it easy to find a job in this career, or is it hard?

You *want* to know this! Believe me, you *want* to know this! Especially if, in order to prepare for this career that interests you, it's going to take some time for you to go get some schooling, or perhaps a degree.

If you fail to ask such questions *ahead of time* you may be bitterly disappointed after you get all that training, or that degree.

You want to know this, before you start. So, *puh-leeze*, talk to people in the career you find so appealing, and ask them these questions I have just suggested. *Please!*

Ask at least three people in that career field those questions.

Make up your own mind whether this is one of 'the *hottest* careers of the '90s.' Don't believe what lists, experts, or well-meaning friends try to claim is a good career *for you*. Test it, make up your own mind. And don't go get a degree because you think that will guarantee you a job! No, mon ami, it will not.

I wish you could see my mail, filled with bitter letters from people who believed such lists as you have just seen, went and got a degree in that field, thought it would be a snap to find a job, but are still unemployed after two years. You would weep! They are bitter (often), angry (always), and disappointed in a society which they feel lied to them.

They found there was no job that went with that degree. They feel lied to, by our society and by the experts, about the value of going back to school, and getting a degree in this or that 'hot' field.

Now that they have that costly worthless degree, and still can't find a job, they find a certain irony in the phrase, "*Our country believes in getting a job by degrees.*"

If you already made this costly mistake, you know what I mean.

A FINAL WORD
ABOUT CHANGING CAREERS

Well, you've ploughed your way through this chapter, and maybe you're thinking: "*Well, I want to change careers. But perhaps this just isn't the right time.*"

Friend, there will never be *a right time*. Conditions will always be *difficult*. Obstacles will always be *in your way*, which you must overcome. It will always be a challenge, should you decide to launch out into the deep and mysterious destiny to which you feel called, by the long-lost dreams of your soul.

By the way, if you're sharing your life with someone, please be sure to take them into your confidence. Sit down with that partner or spouse and ask what the implications are *for them* if you try this new thing. How do they feel about what you're about to do? What will it cost the two of you? Will it require all your joint savings? Will they have to give up things, along with you? If so, what? Are they willing to make those sacrifices? And so on.

If you aren't out of work, you will wrestle with the question of whether you should quit your present job, before you start up this new career.

The experts say that if you have a job, *don't* quit it. Better by far to move *gradually* into your new career, if that is at all possible -- doing it as a moonlighting activity at first, while you are still holding down that regular job somewhere else. That way, you can test out your new adventure, as you would test a floor-board in an old run-down house, stepping on it cautiously without yet putting your full weight on it, to see whether or not it will support you.[14]

Be sure to do your research first, weigh the risks, count the cost, get counsel from those intimately involved with you, and then if you decide you want to do it (whatever *it* is), go ahead and try -- no matter what your well-meaning but pessimistic acquaintances may say.

Just keep these three rules in mind:

---

1. There is always some risk, in trying something new. Your job is not to avoid risk -- there is no way to do that -- but to make sure ahead of time that the risks are *manageable.*

2. You find this out before you start, by first talking to others who have already done what you are thinking of doing; then you evaluate whether or not you still want to go ahead and try it.

3. Have a Plan B, already laid out, *before you start,* as to what you will do if it doesn't work out; i.e., know where you are going to go, next. Don't wait, p*uh-leaze!* Write it out, now. *This is what I'm going to do, if this doesn't work out:* _____

---

14. See Philip Holland, *How To Start A Business Without Quitting Your Job: The Moonlight Entrepreneur's Guide.* Ten Speed Press, Post Office Box 7123, Berkeley, CA 94707. 1992.

These rules always apply, no matter where you are in your life: just starting out, already employed, unemployed, in mid-life, recovering after a crisis or accident, facing retirement, or whatever. Do take them very seriously.

And, *good luck!* In some ways this is a journey in which you cannot fail. Even if you are not able to *pull it off,* in any way that the world calls 'successful,' you will at the very least be a better man or woman for having tried. There is something about *adversity* and *challenge* that tests and refines *character,* even as fire tempers steel. A challenge toward growth and change -- willingly accepted -- can often bring out the very best in us.

You have something unique to contribute to this Earth, while you are here. Any journey you take, toward finding out what that is, will be well worth the adventure.

It's not what we have, but what we are,
that makes the poverty or richness of our life.

Phillips Brooks

FOR
THE DETERMINED
JOB-HUNTER
OR
CAREER-CHANGER

The Systematic Approach To
Career-Change
And Job-Hunting

WHAT
SKILLS DO YOU MOST ENJOY
USING?

You Must Figure Out What Kinds of Tasks
You Most Enjoy Doing
and Which of Your Skills
You Most Delight to Use

102

Chapter 5

> The major difference between successful and unsuccessful job-hunters is not some factor out there (such as a tight job-market), but the way they go about their job-hunt.

Yes, and that has always been true! When a job-hunter tells me: *"I can't find a job"* that tells me nothing, until he tells me *how* he has been looking for it. The method one uses, is everything!

The best method, by far, has over the years turned out to be the so-called **creative job-hunting approach**. This method leads to a job for 86 out of every 100 job-hunters who faithfully follow it. Such an effectiveness-rate -- 86% -- is *astronomically higher* than all other job-hunting methods.[1] That's why when nothing else is working for you, this is the method that you will thank your lucky stars for.

This is also the method you must turn to, if you've decided you would like to find a new career -- and you'd prefer not to have to take years out of your life to go back to school and get retrained with a new degree, etc., etc.

But it is only for the *determined* job-hunter. Making a pass at it, only taking a swipe at it, trying to do it in just a day and a night, will not do. If, to paraphrase an old hymn, *you want to be carried to your job on flowery beds of ease,* this is not the method for you. It requires dedication, determination, time, and hard work -- as most good things in life do. But if you are a *determined* job-hunter or career-changer, you certainly can do it, as millions have before you.

The creative approach to career-change has three parts to it. These parts are in the form of our old familiar questions: *What, Where,* and *How,* here more fully defined:

• WHAT?

The full question here is *what are the skills you most enjoy using?*

To answer this question, you need to identify or inventory what **skills/gifts/talents** you have; and then you need to prioritize them, in their order of importance and enjoyment for you. Experts call these 'transferable skills,' because they are transferable to any field/career that you choose, regardless of where you first picked them up, or how long you've had them.

---

1. I speak of individual job-hunting strategies. Group strategies, such as Nathan Azrin's 'job-club' concept, Chuck Hoffman's Self-Directed Job-Search, Dean Curtis' Group Job Search program, etc., have achieved success-rates in the 85–90% range, using telephone approaches to employers.

> ## • WHERE?
>
> The full question here is *where do you most want to use those skills?*
>
> This has to do *primarily* with the **fields of knowledge** *you have already acquired,* which you most enjoy using. But *where* also has to do with your preferred working conditions, what kinds of data or people or things you enjoy working with, etc.

> ## • HOW?
>
> The full question here is *how do you find such jobs, that use your favorite skills and your favorite fields of knowledge?*
>
> To answer this question, you need to do some **interviewing of various people in order to find the information you are looking for**. You begin this interviewing with the awareness that *skills* point toward job-titles; and *knowledges* point toward a career *field,* where you would use those skills. You want also to find out the names of *organizations* in your preferred geographical area which have such jobs to offer. *And,* the names of the people or person there who actually has the *power* to hire you, as well as the challenges they face. You then secure an interview with them, by using your contacts, and show them how your skills can help them with their challenges.

With this overview in mind, we must now go through each of these three steps in greater detail. This chapter deals with WHAT? Chapter 6 deals with WHERE? And Chapter 7 deals with HOW?

THE CRUCIAL IMPORTANCE
OF "WHAT?"

When you first approach the job-hunt, if you are normal you will instinctively want to leap over *What* and *Where*, and go directly to *How*. You know: *how* do we find vacancies, *how* do we do our resume, *how* do we conduct an interview? There is, in fact, a vast industry in this country and many others, dedicated to conducting workshops that teach people only the *How* part of the job-hunt: resumes, interviews, salary negotiation.

This is a *huge* mistake.

I will explain *why*. Suppose I ask you to look around your house to see if you can find some minor object that is of interest to your cousin Ned, twice-removed, whom you don't much like. Since this assignment is of close to zero interest to you, you can imagine the listless way in which you might go hunting for that object. You'd do the search because you're a good-hearted person, but you'd give it *just a lick and a promise.*

Now, suppose there is some other object in your house, and this one is a beloved object, the only thing left to you by your dear departed grandmother, and you have been hunting for it, in vain, for years. It is *tremendously* important to you. And now I tell you that I saw it, somewhere in the house, just the other day, but can't remember exactly where. Armed with this fresh evidence that it still exists, you can imagine that you'd practically tear that house apart, to find this thing you care about so much, and have been looking for, for years.

The moral of our tale, you've already guessed: *the fervor of your hunt will be directly proportional to how much you care about* **WHAT** *you are hunting for.* That's true in life. It's true also in job-hunting.

THE POWER OF THE VISION

You can now understand why I say: I can teach you all the techniques, job-hunting tricks, and shortcuts in the world, but if your definition of *what you're looking for* leaves you cold, the techniques will be purely academic. You'll likely figure out some way unconsciously to botch them up, to do them incorrectly, to do them half-heartedly, all the while unaware that this is what you're doing. And if you botch them up, it will be for a very healthy reason: your soul does not want *to settle for* anything less than its destiny.

The Secret of Job-Hunting Success
It's an old rule, which you must never forget: Search for a job you only half-care about, and you'll search for it with only half your being; but search for a job you are desperately anxious to find, and you'll hunt for it with all of your being. The more you die to find a particular thing that you most love to do, the more you will alter not only your job-hunt, but your life. Determination is born from Vision, Vision, burning bright.

No matter what other people tell you, you don't increase your job-hunting success by memorizing a few more techniques, a few better answers to an employer's interview questions. You increase your success by working on your vision for your life. By asking yourself: Why am I not happier? What is it that I most want to be doing with my life? What vision, what hunches, what yearnings, do I have about why I was put here, on earth? What are my unfulfilled dreams?

Let's face it, dear reader, you aren't getting any younger. If you don't go after your dreams *now*, when will you?

Now is the time to fulfill your dreams and your vision that you once had of what your life could be. Even if it means hard work. Even if it means changing careers. Even if means going out into the unknown, and taking risks. Manageable risks.

You may think this is a selfish activity -- but it is not. It is related to what *the world most needs* from you. That world currently is *filled* with workers whose weeklong motto is, *When is the weekend going to be here?* And, then, **T**hank **G**od **I**t's **F**riday! They are bored out of their skulls. Some of them are bored because even though they know what they'd rather be doing, they can't get out of their deadend jobs, for one reason or another.

But too many others, unfortunately, are bored simply because they have *never* taken the time to *think* -- to think out what they uniquely can do, and what they uniquely have to offer to the world. They've flopped from one job to another, letting accident, circumstance, coincidence, and whim carry them where it will.

What the world most needs from you is not to add to their number, but to figure out, and then contribute to the world, what you came into this world to do.

It's time for you to fulfill your destiny.

Dust off those dreams.

Let the vision burn brightly! And let it beckon you on.

Then you'll have a job-hunt that truly sets your heart on fire!

HOW DO YOU BEGIN?

You begin this systematic approach -- whether you're just doing a normal job-hunt or you want this to be a full-fledged career-change -- in exactly the same way: by first of all identifying your skills.

Now, many people just "freeze" when they hear the word "skills." It begins with high school job-hunters: "I haven't really got any skills," they say. It continues with college students: "I've spent four years in college. I haven't had time to pick up any

Panel 1: WHY COULDN'T YOU TELL YOUR CAREER COUNSELOR WHAT YOUR GOAL IN LIFE IS, CATHY.? / I DON'T **KNOW** WHAT IT IS.

Panel 2: WHEN I WAS IN GRADE SCHOOL, MY GOAL WAS TO GRADUATE... IN HIGH SCHOOL, MY GOAL WAS TO GRADUATE... IN COLLEGE MY GOAL WAS TO GRADUATE.

Panel 3: SO WHAT ?? IT'S TIME TO SET NEW GOALS !! / IT ISN'T THAT EASY, ANDREA.

Panel 4: I RAN OUT OF THINGS TO GRADUATE FROM.

skills." And it lasts through the middle years, especially when a person is thinking of changing his or her career: "I'll have to go back to college, and get retrained, because otherwise I won't have any skills in my new field." Or: "Well, if I claim any skills, I'll start at a very entry kind of level." All of this fright about the word "skills" is very common, and stems from a total misunderstanding of what the word means. A misunderstanding that is shared, we might add, by altogether too many employers, personnel or human resources departments, and other so-called "vocational experts."

By understanding the word, you will automatically put yourself way ahead of most job-hunters. And, especially if you are weighing a change of career, you can save yourself much waste of time on the folly called "I can only change careers by going back to school for extensive retraining." I've said it before, and I'll say it again: *maybe* you need some retraining, but very often it is possible to make a dramatic career-change without any re-training. It all depends. And you won't really *know* if you need further schooling, until you have finished all the exercises in this and the next chapter.

THE MOST MISUNDERSTOOD
WORD IN THE WORLD OF WORK:
SKILLS

You begin career-change (or a thorough job-hunt) by first identifying your transferable, functional, skills. Here you are looking for what you may think of as the basic building-blocks of your work.

'*. . . and give me good abstract-reasoning ability, interpersonal skills, cultural perspective, linguistic comprehension, and a high sociodynamic potential.*'

The skills you need to inventory, for yourself, are called functional or transferable skills. Here is a famous diagram of them:

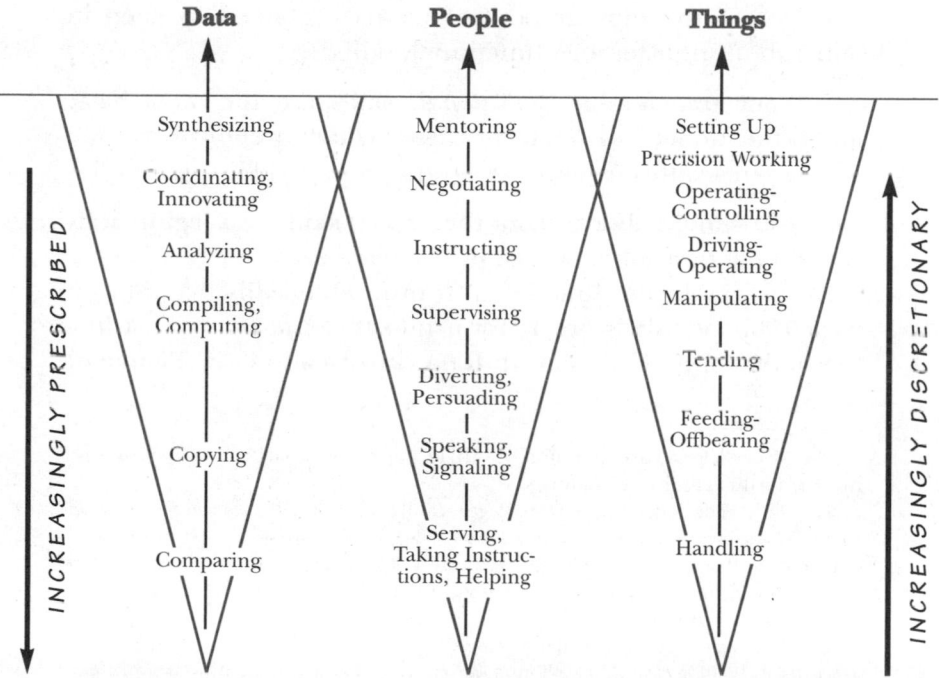

Data	People	Things
Synthesizing	Mentoring	Setting Up
		Precision Working
Coordinating, Innovating	Negotiating	Operating-Controlling
Analyzing	Instructing	Driving-Operating
Compiling, Computing	Supervising	Manipulating
	Diverting, Persuading	Tending
Copying	Speaking, Signaling	Feeding-Offbearing
Comparing	Serving, Taking Instructions, Helping	Handling

INCREASINGLY PRESCRIBED

INCREASINGLY DISCRETIONARY

That's what skills are. Most people, however, think skills are such things as: *has lots of energy, gives attention to details, gets along well with people, shows determination, works well under pressure, is sympathetic, intuitive, persistent, dynamic, dependable,* etc. Despite popular misconceptions, these are not functional/transferable skills, but the *style* with which you do your transferable skills. For example, let's take *"gives attention to details."* If one of your *transferable skills* is *"conducting research"* then *"gives attention to details"* describes the manner or style with which you do that transferable skill called *conducting research.* These phrases which identify *your style* of doing things are commonly called your **traits, temperaments**, or **type.** Popular tests, such as the *Myers-Briggs,* measure this sort of thing.[2]

A CRASH COURSE ON
TRANSFERABLE SKILLS

All right, then, if transferable skills are the heart of your vision and your destiny, let's see just exactly what transferable skills *are.*

Here are the most important truths you need to keep in mind about transferable, functional, skills:

1. Your transferable *(functional)* **skills are the most basic unit -- the atoms -- of whatever career you may choose.**

You can see this from the diagram on page 111.

2. You should always claim the *highest* **skills you legitimately can, on the basis of your past performance.**

As we saw in the functional/transferable skills diagram on page 109, your skills break down into three *families,* according to whether you use them with **Data (Information)**, or **People** or

---

2. The Myers-Briggs Type Indicator, or 'MBTI,' measures what is called *psychological type.* For further reading about this, see:

Paul D. Tieger & Barbara Barron-Tieger, *Do What You Are: Discover the Perfect Career for You Through the Secrets of Personality Type.* 1992. Little, Brown & Company, Inc., division of Time Warner Inc., 34 Beacon St., Boston MA 02108. For those who cannot obtain the MBTI, this book includes a method for readers to identify their personality types. This is a very popular book.

David Keirsey and Marilyn Bates, *Please Understand Me: Character & Temperament Types.* 1978. Includes the Keirsey Temperament Sorter -- again, for those who cannot obtain the MBTI® (Myers-Briggs Type Indicator) -- registered trademarks of Consulting Psychologists Press.

A publication list of other readings about psychological type can be obtained from the Center for Application of Psychological Type, 2720 N.W. 6th St., Gainesville, FL 32609. 904-375-0160.

Skills as The Basic Unit of Work

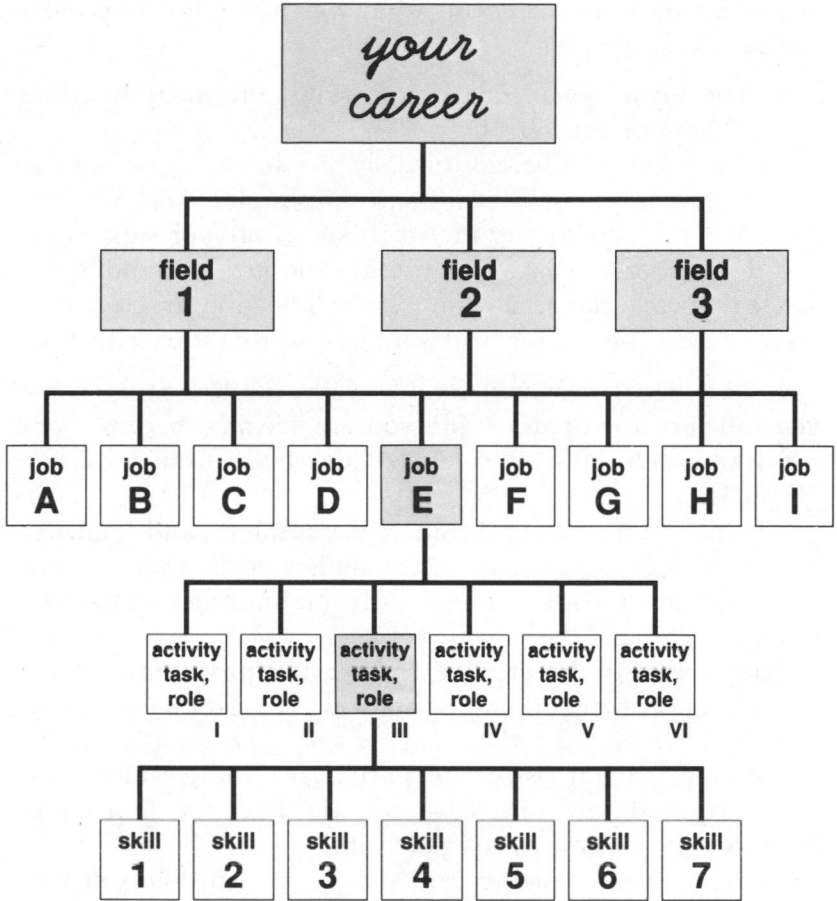

Things. And again, as that diagram makes clear, within each family there are *simple* skills, and there are higher, or *more complex* skills, so that these can be listed as vertical pyramids, with the simpler skills at the bottom, and the more complex ones in order above it, as in the diagram.

Incidentally, as a general rule -- to which there are exceptions -- each *higher* skill requires you to be able also to do all those skills listed below it, on the diagram. So of course you can usually claim *those,* as well. But you want to particularly claim the highest skill you legitimately can, on each transferable skills pyramid, based on what you have already proven you can do in the past.[3]

3. The higher your transferable skills, the more freedom you will have on the job.

Simpler skills can be, and usually are, heavily *prescribed* (by the employer), so if you claim *only* the simpler skills, you will have to *'fit in'* -- following the instructions of your supervisor, and doing exactly what you are told. The *higher* the skills you can legitimately claim, the more you will be given discretion to carve out the job the way you want to -- so that it truly fits *you.*

4. The higher your transferable skills, the less competition you will face for whatever job you are seeking, because jobs which use such skills will rarely be advertised through normal channels.

Not for you the way of classified ads, resumes, and agencies. No, if you can legitimately claim higher skills, then to find such jobs you *must* follow the creative job-hunting methods described in this and the next two chapters.

The essence of this creative approach to job-hunting or career-change is that you may approach *any organization that interests you, whether or not they have a known vacancy.* Naturally, whatever place you visit -- and particularly those which have not advertised any vacancy -- you will find far fewer job-hunters that you have to compete with.

In fact, if the employers you visit happen to like you well enough, they may be willing to create for you a job that does not presently exist. *In which case, you will be competing with no one, since you will be the sole applicant for that newly created job.* While this doesn't happen all the time, it is astounding to me how many times it *does* happen. *The reason* it does is that the employers often have been *thinking* about creating a new job within their organization, for quite some time -- but with this

---

3. If you desire more explanation of what these skills are, I refer you in the U.S. to *The Dictionary of Occupational Titles,* the 1991 revised fourth edition, pp. 1005–1006 in vol. II. It should be available in any public library in the U.S. Other countries (such as Canada) have similar dictionaries.

and that, they just have never gotten around to *doing* it. Until they saw you.

Then they decided they didn't want to let you get away, since *good employees are as hard to find as are good employers.* And they suddenly remember that job they have been thinking about creating for many weeks or months, now. So they dust off their *intention,* create the job on the spot, and offer it to you! And if that new job is not only what *they* need, but is exactly what *you* were looking for, then you have: Match-match. Win-win.

From our country's perspective, it is also interesting to note this: by this job-hunting initiative of yours, you have helped *accelerate* the creation of more jobs in your country, which is so much on everybody's mind here in the '90s. How nice to help your country, as well as yourself!

> And so, the paradoxical moral of all this: The less you try to 'stay loose' and open to *anything,* the more you define your skills with *Data/Information* and/or *People* and/or *Things* in detail, and at the highest level you legitimately can, **the more likely you are to find a job.** *Just the opposite of what the typical career-changer starts out believing.*

"I WOULDN'T RECOGNIZE MY SKILLS IF THEY CAME UP AND SHOOK HANDS WITH ME"

Well, now that you know what skills technically *are,* the problem is figuring out your own. If you are one of the few lucky people who already know what your transferable skills are, blessed are you. Write them down, and put them in the order of preference, for you.

If, however, you don't know what your skills are (and 95% of all workers *don't*), then you will need some help. That help is to be found in *The Parachute Workbook* on page 7.

It involves writing seven stories from your life.

Here is a specific example of such a story, so you can see how it is done:

"I wanted to be able to take a summer trip with my wife and four children. I had a very limited budget, and could not afford to put my family up, in motels. I decided to rig our station wagon as a camper.

"First I went to the library to get some books on campers. I read those books. Next I designed a plan of what I had to build, so that I could outfit the inside of the station wagon, as well as topside. Then I went and purchased the necessary wood. On weekends, over a period of six weeks, I first constructed, in my driveway, the shell for the 'second story' on my station wagon. Then I cut doors, windows, and placed a six-drawer bureau within that shell. I mounted it on top of the wagon, and pinioned it in place by driving two-by-fours under the station wagon's rack on top. I then outfitted the inside of the station wagon, back in the wheelwell, with a table and a bench on either side, that I made.

"The result was a complete homemade camper, which I put together when we were about to start our trip, and then disassembled after we got back home. When we went on our summer trip, we were able to be on the road for four weeks, yet stayed within our budget, since we didn't have to stay at motels.

"I estimate I saved $1900 on motel bills, during that summer's vacation."

Ideally, each story you write should have the following parts, as illustrated above:

I.) **Your goal: what you wanted to accomplish:** *"I wanted to be able to take a summer trip with my wife and four children."*

II.) **Some kind of hurdle, obstacle, or constraint that you faced** (self-imposed or otherwise): *"I had a very limited budget, and could not afford to put my family up, in motels."*

III.) **A description of what you did, step by step** (how you set about to ultimately achieve your goal, above, in spite of this hurdle or constraint): *"I decided to rig our station wagon as a camper. First I went to the library to get some books on campers. I read those books. Next I designed a plan of what I had to build, so that I could outfit the inside of the station wagon, as well as topside. Then I went and purchased the necessary wood. On weekends, over a period of six weeks, I . . ." etc., etc.*

IV.) **A description of the outcome or result:** *"When we went on our summer trip, we were able to be on the road for four weeks, yet stayed within our budget, since we didn't have to stay at motels."*

V.) **Any measurable/quantifiable statement of that outcome, that you can think of:** *"I estimate I saved $1900 on motel bills, during that summer's vacation."*

The Parachute Workbook will take you through the whole process of analyzing seven such stories, identifying your transferable skills therein, and prioritizing them.

Once you have identified your eight top favorite transferable skills *(or however many you wish),* you need to *flesh out* your skill-description for each of those eight, so that you are able to describe each of your talents or skills with more than just a one-word verb or gerund, like: *organizing.*

Let's take *organizing* as our example. You tell us proudly: "I'm good at *organizing.*" That's a fine start at defining your skills, but unfortunately it doesn't yet tell us much. Organizing WHAT? *People,* as at a party? *Nuts and bolts,* as on a workbench? Or *lots of information,* as on a computer? These are three entirely different skills. The one word *organizing* doesn't tell us which one is *yours.*

An Overview of This Process

PUT THEM IN CATEGORIES

△ PEOPLE □ THINGS ○ DATA

△ PEOPLE □ THINGS ○ DATA

PRIORITIZE THEM ACCORDING TO ENJOYMENT

So, please *flesh out* each of your favorite transferable skills with an object -- some kind of *Data/Information,* or some kind of *People,* or some kind of *Thing,* and then add an adverb or adjective, too.

Why adjectives? Well, "I'm good at organizing information *painstakingly and logically*" and "I'm good at organizing information *in a flash, by intuition,*" are two *entirely different* skills. The difference between them is spelled out not in the verb, nor in the object, but in the adjectival or adverbial phrase there at the end. So, expand each definition of your eight favorite skills, in the fashion I have just described.

> When you are face-to-face with a person-who-has-the-power-to-hire-you, you want to be able to explain what makes you different from nineteen other people who can basically do the same thing that you can do. It is often the adjective or adverb that will save your life, during that explanation.

A PICTURE IS WORTH A THOUSAND WORDS

When you have your eight top favorite skills, in order, and *fleshed out,* it is time to put them on the central petal of the diagram, which we call *The Flower Diagram,* that you will find on page 75.

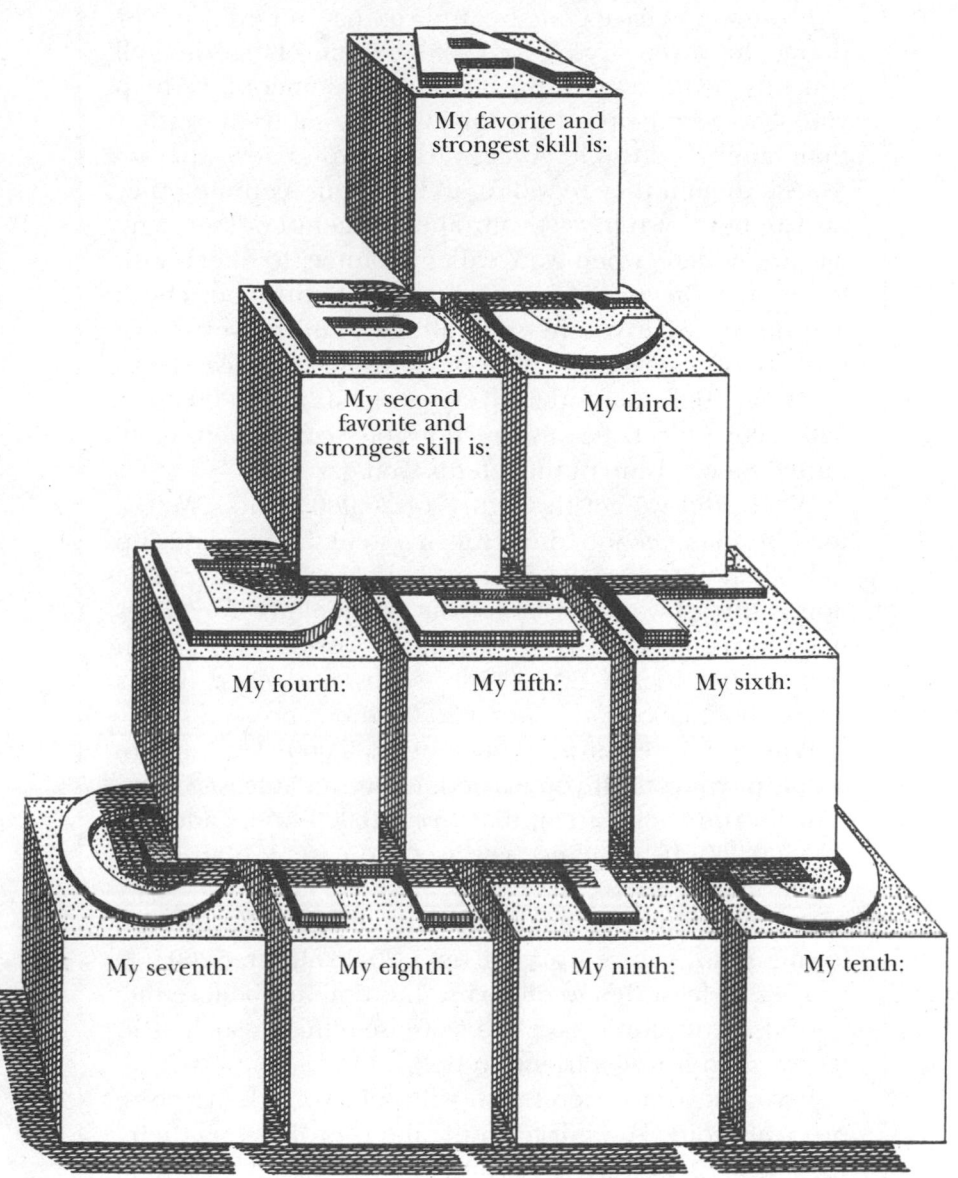

You may also, or alternatively, want to enroll them on the building-block diagram here -- in which case, you can list your top ten. And that's it, for this chapter.

Voila! You now have finished with **WHAT**.

A Friendly Word to Procrastinators

If two weeks have gone by, and you haven't even *started* doing the inventory of your skills, then -- I hate to tell you this -- you're going to have to get someone to help you. Choose a helper for your job-hunt -- a friend rather than family, if possible. A *tough* friend. You know, *taskmaster*. Ask them if they're willing to help you. Assuming they say yes, put down in *both* your appointment books a regular *weekly* date when you will guarantee to meet with them, and they will guarantee to meet with you, check you out on what you've done already, and be very stern with you if you've done little or nothing since last week's meeting. Tell them that it is at least a 20,000-hour, $200,000 project. It's also responsible, concerned, committed Stewardship of the talents God gave you.

Where did we get the figure of 20,000 hours? Well, a forty-hour-a-week job, done for fifty weeks a year, adds up to 2,000 hours annually. So, how long are you going to be doing this new career that you are looking for? How many years do you plan to stay in the world of work? Ten years? That means 20,000 hours. Twenty years? That's 40,000 hours. So, it's at least a 20,000-hour project.

Where did we get the figure of $200,000? Well, figure it out for yourself. If you earned, let us say, at least $10 an hour in your new career, that *times* 20,000 hours adds up to $200,000. If by chance you were to earn $20 an hour, that would be $400,000.

So, in working through this chapter and the two following ones, you're working on a 20,000-hour, $200,000 project, at least. It's *worth* giving the time to, believe me.

And if you don't have the self-discipline to stick at it, it's worth enlisting a friend to help you.

If you have no friend who will help you, then you're probably going to want to think about professional help. (See pages *249 ff*, in *The Resource Guide*). Go talk to several career-counselors. Choose the one you like best, and *get on with it*.

You've only one life to live, my friend. And every day is precious.

"Same career, change of career, same career . . . change of . . ."

Chapter Five Postscript
SOME PROBLEMS YOU MAY RUN INTO, WHILE DOING YOUR SKILL-IDENTIFICATION

In doing the aforementioned skill-identification, it will not be surprising if you run into some problems. Let us look at the five more common ones that have arisen for job-hunters, in the past:

1. "I don't know exactly what is an achievement."

When you're looking for a story/achievement to illustrate one of your skills, you're *not* looking for something that only you have done, in the history of the world. What you're looking for is a lot simpler than that. You're looking for *any* time in your life when you did something that was, at that time of your life, a source of pride and accomplishment *for you*. It might have been learning to ride a bike. It might be achieving your first quota, at work. It might be a particularly significant project that you designed, in mid-life. It doesn't matter whether or not it pleased anybody else; it only matters that it pleased you.

I like Bernard Haldane's definition of an achievement. He says it is: something you yourself feel you have done well, that you also enjoyed doing and felt proud of. In other words you are looking for an accomplishment which gave you two pleasures: enjoyment while doing it, and satisfaction from the outcome. That doesn't mean you may not have sweated as you did it, or hated *some parts* of the process, but it does mean that basically you enjoyed *most of* the process. The pleasure was not simply in getting it done. Generally speaking, an achievement will have all the parts outlined on page 115.

2. "I don't see why I should look for skills I enjoy; it seems to me that employers will only want to know what skills I do well. They will not care whether I enjoy using the skill or not."

Well, sure, it is important for you to find the skills you do well, above all else. But, generally speaking, that is hard for you to evaluate about yourself. *Do I do this well, or not? Compared to whom?* Even aptitude tests can't resolve this dilemma for you. So it's better to take the following circular equation, which experience has shown to be true:

If it is a skill you do well, you will generally enjoy it.

If it is a skill you enjoy, it is generally because you do it well.

With these equations in hand, you will see that -- since they are equal anyway -- it is much more useful to ask yourself, "Do I enjoy doing it?" instead of hunting for the elusive "Do I do it well?" I repeat: listing the skills you most *enjoy* is -- in most cases -- just another way of listing the skills you do *best*.

The reason why this idea -- of making *enjoyment* the key -- causes such feelings of uncomfortableness in so many of us is that we have an old historical tradition in this country which insinuates you shouldn't really enjoy yourself in life. To suffer is virtuous.

Sample: Two girls do babysitting. One hates it. One enjoys it thoroughly. Which is more virtuous in God's sight? According to that old tradition, the one who hates it is more virtuous. Some of us feel this instinctively, even if more logical thought says, Whoa!

We have this subconscious fear that if we are caught enjoying life, punishment looms. Thus, the story of two Scotchmen who met on the street one day: "Isn't this a beautiful day?" said one. "Aye," said the other, "but we'll pay for it."

We feel it is okay to talk about our failures, but not about our successes. To talk about our successes appears to be boasting, and that is manifestly a sin. Or so we think. We shouldn't be enjoying so much about ourselves.

But look at the birds of the air, or watch your pets at play. You will notice one distinctive fact about that part of God's creation: when a bird or a pet does what it is meant to do, by God and nature, it manifests true joy.

Joy is so clearly a part of God's plan for us. God wants us to eat; therefore He made eating enjoyable. God wants us to sleep; therefore He made sleeping enjoyable. God wants us to procreate, love, and make love; therefore He made sex enjoyable, and love even more so.

Likewise, God gives to each of us unique combinations of skills and talents which He wants us to contribute to His general plan -- to the symphony of the world, and the music of the spheres. Therefore, **when we use the talents He most wants each of us to use, He attends it with a feeling of great joy.** Everywhere in God's plan for His creation, joy rewards right action.

You need to identify the skills you enjoy using -- not only now, as you are in the process of choosing a new career, but also later when you are face-to-face with an employer. True, bad employers will not care whether you enjoy a particular task, or not. But good employers will care greatly. They know that unless a would-be employee has **enthusiasm** for his or her work, the quality of that work will always suffer.

3. "I have no difficulty finding stories to write up, from my life, that I consider to be enjoyable achievements; but once these are written, I have great difficulty in seeing what the skills are -- even if I stare at the skills keys diagram for hours. I need somebody else's insight."

You will want to consider getting two friends or two other members of your family to sit down with you, and do skill identification through the practice of 'Trioing' which I invented some twenty years ago to help with this very problem. This practice is fully described in my book, *Where Do I Go From Here With My Life?* But to save you the trouble of reading it, here is -- in general -- how it goes:

a. Each of the three of you quietly writes up some story of an accomplishment in their life that was enjoyable.

b. Each of the three of you quietly analyzes just your own story to see what skills you see there; you jot these down.

c. One of you then volunteers to go first. You read your story aloud. The other two jot down on a piece of paper whatever skills they hear you using. They ask you to pause if they're having trouble keeping up. You finish your story. You read aloud the skills *you* picked out in that story.

d. Then the second person tells you what's on their list: what skills *they* heard you use in your story. You copy them down, below your own list, even if you don't agree with every one of them.

e. Then the third person tells you what's on their list; what skills *they* heard you use in your story. You copy them down, below your own list, even if you don't agree with every one of them.

f. When they're both done, you ask them any questions for further elaboration that you may have. *"What did you mean by this skill? Where did you think you heard me using it?"*

g. Now it is the next person's turn, and you repeat steps 'c' through 'f' with them. Then it is the third person's turn, and you repeat steps 'c' through 'f' with them.

h. Now it is time to move on to a second story for each of you, so you begin with steps 'a' through 'g' all over again, except that each of you writes a new story. And so on, through seven stories.

4. *"How do I know if I've done this all correctly? What if I just think I understood what I was supposed to do, but I really didn't? I want to be sure the stuff I've identified is really going to help me in my job-hunt."*

It will, if you've followed *all* the directions in *The Parachute Workbook* plus this chapter *(no shortcuts)* and *if* you avoided stating your skills in the jargon or language of your past career, such as the military or the clergy. It is not useful to state your transferable skills in the jargon of your old profession, such as, *"I am good at preaching."* If you are going to choose a new career, out there in what you call the secular world, you must not use language that locks you into the past -- or suggests that you were good in one field and one field only. Therefore, it is important to take *preaching* and ask yourself what is its larger form? *"Teaching?"* Perhaps. *"Motivating people?"* Perhaps. *"Inspiring people to the depths of their being?"* Perhaps. *Only you can say what is true, for you.* But in one way or another be sure to get your skills out of *any jargon that locks you into your past career.*

5. *Do you have any final advice, for me while I'm doing skill-identification?*

Yes. Once you've finished your skill-identification, steer clear of prematurely putting a job-title on the skills you see. In actual fact, skills can point to *many* different jobs, which have a multitude of titles, as you will see in the next chapter. Therefore, don't lock yourself in, prematurely. *"I'm looking for a job where I can use the following skills,"* is fine. But, *"I'm looking for a job where I can be a (job-title)"* is a no-no, at this point in your job-hunt. *Narrowing down* will come later; but at this point, keep *all* your options open.

TRAVELS WITH FARLEY by Phil Frank © 1982. Field Enterprises, Inc. Courtesy of Field Newspaper Syndicate.

In case you feel, after all of this, you just can't do the stories, you will be interested in this account from a woman job-hunter in England, who wrote me as follows:

"I have a Ph.D. in Chemistry, but the last thing I wanted to do on graduating was to work in a laboratory or a research group. I read your book, and tried -- but failed -- to write the stories; it required too much soul-searching! Consequently, it took me nine months before I decided on a new career path. It was Daniel Porot's PIE method that got me there -- Practice Interviewing, Informational Interviewing, Employment Interviewing. It helped build my confidence enormously, and I felt I had the power -- rather than being the victim of the employment market. I followed your ideas and advice, and have just been offered my first permanent position. I am overjoyed, because I chose this new career looking at my interests and skills, rather than my qualifications. Now I am a Clinical Research Scientist in a hospital. I feel now at long last, at 27 years of age, I am finally on the right track to finding my mission in life."

*A realist is more correct about things
in life than an optimist. But the
optimist seems to have more friends
and much more fun.*[1]

Megan, Age 14

The latest self-help book for pessimists

---

1. From H. Jackson Brown, Jr.'s *When You Lick a Slug, Your Tongue Goes Numb: Kids share their wit and wisdom.* Rutledge Hill Press, Nashville, Tennessee. 1994. Used with permission.

FOR THE DETERMINED JOB-HUNTER OR CAREER-CHANGER

The Systematic Approach To Career-Change And Job-Hunting

WHERE

DO YOU MOST WANT TO USE THOSE SKILLS?

You Must Figure Out Just Exactly What Field and What Kinds of Places You Would Most Delight to Work In

Chapter 6

Table of Contents

THE LANGUAGE OF YOUR CAREER

I once worked as a secretary/typist. That is WHAT I did. But, of course, I had a lot of choices about WHERE I did it.

I could have worked as a legal secretary, or as a secretary at a gardening store, or as a secretary at an airline, or as a secretary at a church, or as a secretary at a photographic laboratory, or as a secretary at a bank, or as a secretary at a chemical plant, or as a secretary in the Federal government.

The point I am making is: it is not sufficient to simply say WHAT you want to do: *I want to be a secretary.* You must define for yourself WHERE you want to do that kind of work. These various places where you *might* work as a secretary -- law, gardening, airlines, church, photography, banking, chemistry, or government, etc., etc. -- are commonly called **Majors**, or **Subjects**, or **Fields**, or **Fields of interest**, or **Fields of knowledge**.

There is, however, another way of thinking about them, and that is as if they were *languages.* If you're puzzled as to what field you would like to be in, for your next career or job, begin by asking yourself what *language* or *languages* you love to listen to, speak, and work in, all day long.

If you work as a legal secretary, you'll have to endure a lot of talk there, all day long, about legal procedures. Therefore, Law is the *language* you have to live with, every day, at that workplace. Do you like that *language?* If so, choose law as your field -- for your next career or job.

Again, if you work as a secretary at a gardening store, there's a lot of talk there, all day long, about gardens and such. Therefore, Gardening is the *language* you have to live with, all day, at that workplace. Do you like that *language?* If so, choose horticulture as your field -- for your next career or job.

If you work as a secretary at an airline, there's a lot of talk there, all day long, about airlines procedures. Therefore, Airlines is the *language* you have to live with, all day, at that workplace. Do you like that *language?* If so, choose air transportation as your field -- for your next career or job.

If you work as a secretary at a church, there's a lot of talk there, all day long, about church procedures and matters of faith. Therefore, Religion is the *language* you have to live with, all day, at that workplace. Do you like that *language?* If so, choose religion as your field -- for your next career or job.

If you work as a secretary in a photographic laboratory, there's a lot of talk there, all day long, about photographic procedures. Therefore, Photography is the *language* you have to live with, all day, at that workplace. Do you like that *language?* If so, choose photography as your field -- for your next career or job.

If you work as a secretary at a bank, there's a lot of talk there, all day long, about banking procedures. Therefore, Banking is the *language* you have to live with, all day, at that workplace. Do you like that *language?* If so, choose banking as your field -- for your next career or job.

If you work as a secretary at a chemical plant, there's a lot of talk there, all day long, about chemicals manufacturing. Therefore, Chemistry is the *language* you have to live with, all day, at that workplace. Do you like that *language?* If so, choose chemistry as your field -- for your next career or job.

If you work as a secretary for the Federal government, there's a lot of talk there, all day long, about government procedures. Therefore, Government is the *language* you have to live with, all day, at that workplace. Do you like that *language?* If so, choose government as your field -- for your next career or job.

As a general rule, if you enjoy the *language* you deal with all day, then you will be happy in that field or career.

However, if you don't enjoy the *language* spoken at work -- if, say, *gardening* is your favorite subject, but you work at a place where *law* -- a language you hate -- is what you have to listen to, and work with, all day long, then you are not going to be happy in that career.

WHAT DO YOU LOVE
TO TALK ABOUT OR BE IMMERSED IN?

It is important for you to begin your consideration of "WHERE do I want to use my (favorite) skills?" by making a list of your *Favorite Subjects* (*i.e., languages*). In the case of each *field* or *language* you list, it is only necessary that you love talking about this subject, and know *something* about it -- it is not necessary that you have a *mastery* of it.

Also, it doesn't have to be a subject you studied in school. As I mentioned in Chapter 4, most people think that if they're going to change careers, they have to go back and master some new field at a college, or university. Well, sometimes that's the case; but not always, by any means. Your next career can be in a field that you just picked up along the way in life -- say, *antiques,* or *cars,* or *interior decorating,* or *music* or *movies* or *psychology,* or *the kind of subjects that come up on television 'game shows.'*

The only important thing is that you *like* the subject a lot, and that you picked up a working knowledge of it -- who cares where or how? As the late John Crystal used to say, it doesn't matter whether you learned it in college, or sitting at the end of a log.

Let's take *antiques* as an example. Suppose it's one of your favorite subjects, yet you never studied it in school. You picked up your knowledge of antiques by going around to antique stores, and asking lots of questions. And you supplemented this by reading a few books on the subject, and you subscribe to an antiques magazine. You've also bought a few antiques, yourself. That's enough, for you to put *antiques,* on your list of fields/interests/languages. Your degree of *mastery* of this whole field of antiques is irrelevant -- *unless you want to work at a level in the field that demands and requires* mastery.

THE FLOWER DIAGRAM

How, exactly, do you go about figuring out what your favorite *languages,* i.e., fields, are?

Well, you need a series of checklists, and we have provided these for you, in that part of *The Parachute Workbook* that begins on page *55*.

It will guide you not only through *languages,* but through the whole process of identifying WHERE -- after which, you can enroll what you discover on the *petals* on the Flower Diagram there.

All of this will take you a bit of time, but not more than a few hours, normally.

When you've got all eight *petals* of the *Flower Diagram* filled in (page *75*), you might then want to cut out all eight *petals* -- and paste them together on one large sheet.

Put that sheet on a wall, or on the door of your refrigerator. And there you have it: Your Flower Diagram.

But, what exactly is it that you have there? Well, it's a picture of *you* (sort of) and it's also a picture of *the job or career* you're looking for. It's both these things at once, because you've constructed a picture of a job or career *that matches you.*

A LIGHT BULB
GOES ON

And when you're looking at that diagram, what should happen? Well, for some of you *(about three in every hundred of those reading this book)* there will be a big *Aha!* as you look at your Flower Diagram. A light bulb will go off, over your head, and you will say, "My goodness, I see *exactly* what sort of career this points me to."

If you are one of these extremely intuitive people, I say, "Good for you!" Just two gentle warnings, if I may: don't prematurely close out *other* possibilities. And *don't* say to yourself:

"Well, I see what it is that I would die to be able to do, but I *know* there is no job in the world like that, that *I* would be able to get." Dear friend, you don't know any such thing. You haven't done your research yet.

To be sure, it is possible that when you've completed all that research, and conducted your search, you still may not be able to find *all* that you want -- down to the last detail.

But you'd be surprised at how much of your dream you may be able to find.

Sometimes it will be found in *stages.* One retired man I know, who had been a senior executive with a publishing company, found himself bored to death in retirement, after he turned 65. He contacted a business acquaintance, who said apologetically, "We just don't have anything open that matches or requires your abilities; right now all we need is someone in our mail room." The 65-year-old executive said, "I'll take that job!" He did, and over the ensuing years steadily advanced once again, to just the job he wanted: as a senior executive in that organization, where he utilized all his prized skills, for some time. He retired as senior executive for the second time, at the age of 85.

Other times, you may be able to find your dream, directly, without having to go through stages.

It is amazing how often people do get their dreams, whether in stages or directly. The more you don't *cut* the dream down, because of what you *think* you know about *the real world,* the more likely you are to find what you are looking for.

Most people don't find their heart's desire, because they decide to pursue just half their dream -- and consequently they hunt for it with only *half a heart.*

If you decide to pursue your whole dream, your best dream, the one you die to do, I guarantee you that you will hunt for it *with all your heart.* It is this *passion* which often is the difference between successful career-changers, and unsuccessful ones.

YOU LOOK AT YOUR FLOWER DIAGRAM AND. . . NOTHING!

Most of you will look at your Flower Diagram, and you won't have *a clue* as to what job or career it points to. Soooo, you're going to have to do some additional research, *of course.*

Here's how you begin. Take a pad of paper, with pen or pencil, or go to your computer, keyboard in hand, and make some notes.

First, look at your Flower Diagram, and write down your three to five most *favorite* skills.

Then, look at your Flower Diagram and write down your three to five most *favorite* vocational *languages,* alias *fields of knowledge,* or *fields of interest.*

Take your notes, and show them to at least five friends, family, or professionals whom you know.

> As you will recall from Chapter 4, skills usually point toward a **job-title** or job-level, while fields of interest or knowledge usually point toward a **career field**. So, you want to ask them, in the case of your skills, *What job or jobs do these suggest to you?*
>
> Then ask them, in the case of your favorite vocational *languages, What career fields do these suggest to you?*

Jot down *everything* these five people tell you.

After you have finished talking to them, you want to go home and look at what the five have told you. Incidentally, if none of it looks valuable, go talk to five more of your friends or acquaintances, plus any people you know in the business world and non-profit sector.

When you've got some worthwhile ideas, sit down, look over their combined suggestions, and ask yourself some questions.

• First, you want to look at what they suggested about your skills: *what job or jobs came to their mind?* It will help you to know that most jobs can be classified under 19 headings or families, as listed on the next page.

Which of these nineteen do your friends' suggestions predominantly point to? Which of these nineteen grabs you?

• Next, you want to look at what they suggested about your *favorite languages: what fields or careers came to their mind?* It will help you to know that most career fields can be classified, first of all, under four broad headings: *Agriculture, Manufacturing, Information industries,* and *Service industries.*

Which of these four do your friends' suggestions predominantly *point to?* Which of these four grabs you?

• The next question you want to ask yourself is: both job-titles and career-fields can be broken down further, according to whether you like to work primarily with *people* **or** primarily with *information/data* **or** primarily with *things.*

Let's take agriculture as an example. Within agriculture, you could be driving tractors and other farm machinery -- and thus working primarily with *things;* or you could be gathering

JOB
FAMILIES

1. Executive, Administrative, and Managerial Occupations
2. Engineers, Surveyors, and Architects
3. Natural Scientists and Mathematicians
4. Social Scientists, Social Workers, Religious Workers, and Lawyers
5. Teachers, Counselors, Librarians, and Archivists
6. Health Diagnosing and Treating Practitioners
7. Registered Nurses, Pharmacists, Dieticians, Therapists, and Physician Assistants
8. Health Technologists and Technicians
9. Writers, Artists, and Entertainers
10. Technologists and Technicians, Except Health
11. Marketing and Sales Occupations
12. Administrative Support Occupations, Including Clerical
13. Service Occupations
14. Agricultural, Forestry, and Fishing Occupations
15. Mechanics and Repairers
16. Construction and Extractive Occupations
17. Production Occupations
18. Transportation and Material Moving Occupations
19. Handlers, Equipment Cleaners, Helpers, and Laborers

statistics about crop growth for some state agency -- and thus working primarily with *information/data;* or you could be teaching agriculture in a college classroom, and thus working primarily with *people* and *ideas.* Almost all fields as well as career families offer you these three kinds of choices, though *of course* many jobs combine two or more of the three.

Still, you do want to tell yourself what your *preference* is, and what you *primarily* want to be working with. Otherwise your job-hunt or career-change is going to leave you very frustrated, at the end. In this matter, it is often your favorite skill that will give you the clue. If it *doesn't*, then go back and look at your total skills *petal*, on pages *40–41*. What do you think? Are your favorite skills weighted more toward working with *people*, or toward working with *information/data*, or toward working with *things*?

And, no matter what that *petal* suggests, which do you think you prefer?

THE TRANSCENDENT IMPORTANCE OF PEOPLE

Once you have these *clues* from your friends, you need to go gather some further information. Specifically, you want to find answers to these four WHERE questions, in the sequence indicated:

• QUESTION #1
What are the **names of jobs or careers** that would give me a chance to use my most enjoyable skills, in a field that is based on my favorite subjects?

• QUESTION #2
What **kinds of organizations** would and/or do employ people in these careers?

• QUESTION #3
Among the kinds of organizations uncovered in the previous question, what are the names of **particular places** that I especially like?

• QUESTION #4
Among the places that I particularly like, **what needs do they have** or what outcomes are they trying to produce, that my skills and knowledge could help with?

And how do you find the answers to these four questions? Well, let's begin with the first one; because in seeing how you explore that question, you will understand how to explore the other three, in turn.

The first question is: What are the **names of jobs or careers** that would give me a chance to use my most enjoyable skills, in a field that is based on my favorite subjects?

Where do you begin? The Internet is one place, if you're on the Internet. Libraries are another, if you like to do research in libraries.

The bad news, unfortunately -- for the shy -- is that the most dependable and up-to-date information on jobs and careers is *not* found in either of these two ways. It's found by going and talking to *people*. The reason for this is that last week's absolutely true, certifiably guaranteed, 100% accurate information about jobs and careers is, today, completely outdated. *Things are just moving too fast.* Books can't keep up. They're outdated before they're in print. So, if you want to identify a new career or job that *fits* you, you must go see people -- with *some*

reading on the side, to *supplement* what they tell you. It's no time to be shy!

If shyness is a problem for you, I have a word to say about how to deal with that, at the end of this chapter.

But let us return to our train of thought, here. To gather the information you need, you must go talk to people. Ah, but how do you decide *which people?* Well, it's relatively easy. Let me give you an actual example of how it's done. (We'll take an actual career-changer I've known.)

After doing his Flower Diagram, it turned out that his top/ favorite skill was: diagnosing, treating, or healing.

His three top/favorite *languages* or fields of knowledge were: psychiatry, plants, and carpentry.

After showing five friends this information, and mulling over what they said, he concluded:

Among the 19 *Job families*, he was most attracted to (6) Health diagnosing and treating practitioners.

Among the four *broad divisions of career-fields*, he was most attracted to Service industries.

Among the *three kinds of skills*, he most wanted to use his skills with people.

So far, so good. Now, where does he go from here?

He's going to have to go talk to people. But, how does he choose who to talk to? Easy. He takes his favorite *languages* or fields of knowledge, above -- psychiatry, plants, and carpentry -- and mentally translates them into *people* with particular occupations: namely, a psychiatrist, a gardener, and a carpenter.

Then he has to go find at least one of each. That's relatively easy: the Yellow Pages of the telephone directory will do, or he may know some of these among the friends or acquaintances he already has. What he wants to do, now, is go visit them and ask them: *how do you combine these three fields into one occupation?* He knows it may be a career that already exists, *or* it may be he will have to create this career for himself.

And, how does he decide which of these three to go interview *first?* He asks himself which of these persons is most likely to have the *largest overview. (This is often, but not always, the same as asking: who took the longest to get their training?)* The particular answer here: the psychiatrist.

He would then go see two or three psychiatrists -- say, the heads of the psychiatry departments at the nearest colleges or universities,[2] and ask them: *Do you have any idea how to put these three subjects -- carpentry, plants, and psychiatry -- together into one job or career? And if you don't know, who do you think might?* He would keep going until he found someone who had a bright idea about how you put this all together.

In this particular case *(as I said, this is from an actual career-changer's experience)*, he was eventually told: "Yes, it can all be put together. There is a branch of psychiatry that uses plants to help heal people. That takes care of your interest in plants and psychiatry. As for your carpentry interests, I suppose you could use that to build the planters for your plants."

INFORMATIONAL INTERVIEWING

There is a name for this process I have just described. It is called *Informational Interviewing* -- a term I invented many many years ago. But it is sometimes, incorrectly, called *by other names.* Some even call this gathering of information *Networking,* which it is not.

To avoid this confusion, I have summarized in the chart on the next pages just exactly what *Informational Interviewing* is, and how it differs from the other ways in which *people* can help and support you, during your job-hunt or career-change -- namely, *Networking, Support Groups,* and *Contacts.* I have also thrown in, at no extra charge, a *first* column in that chart, dealing with an aspect of the job-hunt that *never* gets talked about: namely, the importance before your job-hunt ever begins, of *nurturing the friendships you have let slip* -- by calling them or visiting them early on in your job-hunt -- just re-establishing relationships *before* you ever need anything from them, as you most certainly may, later on in your job-hunt. The first column in the chart explains this further.

---

2. If there were no psychiatrists at any academic institution near him, then he would do all his research with psychiatrists in private practice -- getting their names from the phone book -- and asking them for, and paying for, *a half session.* This, if there is no other way.

The Process ▼	1. Valuing Your *Community* Before the Job-Hunt	2. Networking
What Is Its Purpose?	To make sure that people whom you may someday need to do you a favor, or lend you a hand, know long beforehand that you value and prize them *for themselves.*	To gather a list of contacts *now* who might be able to help you with your career, or with your job-hunting, at some future date. And to go out of your way to *regularly* add to that list. *Networking is a term often reserved only for the business of adding to your list; but, obviously, this presupposes you first listed everyone you* already *know.*
Who Is It Done With?	Those who live with you, plus your family, relatives, friends, and acquaintances, however near (geographically) or far.	People in your present field, or in a field of future interest that you yourself meet; also, people whose names are given to you by others.
When You're Doing This Right How Do You Go About It? (Typical Activities)	You make time for them in your busy schedule, long before you find yourself job-hunting. You do this by: (1) Spending 'quality time' with those you live with, letting them know you really appreciate who they are, and what kind of person they are, (2) Maintaining contact (phone, lunch, a thank-you note) with those who live nearby, (3) Writing friendly notes, regularly, to those who live at a distance -- *thus letting them all know that you appreciate them* for themselves.	You deliberately attend, for this purpose, meetings or conventions in your present field, or the field/career you are thinking of switching to, someday. You talk to people at meetings and at 'socials,' exchanging calling cards after a brief conversation. Occasionally, someone may suggest a name to you as you are about to set off for some distant city or place, recommending that while you are there, you contact them. A phone call may be your best bet, with follow-up letter after you return home, unless *they* invite *you* to lunch during the phone call. Asking *them* to lunch sometimes 'bombs.' (See below.)
When You've Really Botched This Up, What Are The Signs?	You're out of work, and you find yourself having to contact people that you haven't written or phoned in ages, suddenly asking them out of the blue for their help with your job-hunt. *The message inevitably read from this is that you don't really care about them at all, except when you can* use *them. Further, you get perceived as one who sees others only in terms of what they can do for you, rather than in a relationship that is 'a two-way street.'*	It's usually when you have approached a very busy individual and asked them to have lunch with you. If it is an aimless lunch, with no particular agenda -- they ask during lunch what you need to talk about, and you lamely say, "Well, uh, I don't know, So-and-So just thought we should get to know each other" -- you will not be practicing *Networking.* You will be practicing *antagonizing.* Try to restrict your *Networking* to the telephone.

Guide To Relationships With Others

3. Developing A Support Group	4. Informational Interviewing	5. Using Contacts
To enlist some of your family or close friends specifically to help you with your emotional, social, and spiritual needs, when you are going through a difficult transition period, such as a job-hunt or career-change -- so that you do not have to face this time all by yourself.	To screen careers *before* you change to them. To screen jobs *before* you take them, rather than afterward. To screen places *before* you decide you want to seek employment there. To find answers to *very specific questions* that occur to you during your job-hunt.	It takes, let us say, 77 pairs of eyes and ears to find a new job or career. Here you recruit those 76 other people (don't take me literally -- it can be any number you choose) to be your eyes and ears -- once you know what kind of work, what kind of place, what kind of job you are looking for, *and not before*.
You try to enlist people with one or more of the following qualifications: you feel comfortable talking to them; they will take initiative in calling you, on a regular basis; they are wiser than you are; and they can be a hard taskmaster, when you need one.	Workers, workers, workers. You *only* do informational interviewing with people actually doing the work that interests you as a potential new job or career for yourself.	Anyone and everyone who is on your 'networking list.' (See column 2.) It includes family, friends, relatives, high school alumni, college alumni, former co-workers, church/synagogue members, places where you shop, etc.
There should be three of them, at least. They may meet with you regularly, once a week, as a group, for an hour or two, to check on how you are doing. One or more of them should also be available to you on an "as needed" basis: the Listener, when you are feeling 'down,' and need to talk; the Initiator, when you are tempted to hide; the Wise One, when you are puzzled as to what to do next; and the Taskmaster, when your discipline is falling apart, and you need someone to encourage you to 'get at it.' It helps if there is also a Cheerleader among them, that you can tell your victories to.	You get names of workers from your co-workers, from departments at local community colleges, or career offices. Once you have names, you call them and ask for a chance to talk to them *for twenty minutes.* You make a list, ahead of time, of all the questions you want answers to. If nothing occurs to you, try these: (1) How did you get into this line of work? Into this particular job? (2) What kinds of things do you like the most about this job? (3) What kinds of things do you like the least about this job? (4) Who else, doing this same kind of work, would you recommend I go talk to?	Anytime you're stuck, you ask your contacts for help *with specific information.* For example: When you can't find workers who are doing the work that interests you. When you can't find the names of places which do that kind of work. When you have a place in mind, but can't figure out the name of 'the person-who-has-the-power-to-hire-you.' When you know that name, but can't get in to see that person. At such times, you call every contact you have on your Networking list, if necessary, until someone can tell you the specific answer you need.
You've 'botched it' when you have no support group, no one to turn to, no one to talk to, and you feel that you are in this, all alone. You've 'botched it' when you are waiting for your friends and family to notice how miserable you are, and to prove they love you by taking the initiative in coming after you; rather than, as is necessary with a support group, *your* choosing and recruiting them -- asking them for their help and aid.	You're trying to use this with people-who-have-the-power-to-hire-you, rather than with *workers.* You're claiming you want information when really you have some other hidden agenda, with this person. *(P.S. They usually can smell the hidden agenda, a mile away.)* You've botched it, whenever you're telling a lie to someone. The whole point of informational interviewing is that it is a search for Truth.	Approaching your 'contacts' too early in your job-hunt, and asking them for help only in the most general and vague terms: "John, I'm out of work. If you hear of anything, please let me know." *Any what thing?* You must do all your own homework *before* you approach your contacts. They will not do your homework for you.

TALKING TO WORKERS,
'TRYING ON' JOBS

Now, when you go talk to people, you are hoping they will give you ideas, as we saw, about *what careers* will use your skills and languages or fields of knowledge and interest.

That's the first step.

The second step is that you want also to get some idea of *what that work feels like, from the inside.*

In the example above, you don't just want the job-title: *psychiatrist working with plants.* You want some feel for the substance that is underneath the title. In other words, you want to find out what the day-to-day work is like.

For this purpose you must leave your *overview people* and go talk to actual living examples of people doing the work you think you'd love: in the particular example we have been discussing, you must go talk to actual *psychiatrists who use plants, in their healing work.*

Why do you want to ask them what the work feels like, from the inside? Well, in effect, you are mentally *trying on jobs* to see if they fit you.

It is exactly analogous to your going to a clothing store and trying on different suits (or dresses) that you see in their window or on their racks. Why do you try them on? Well, the suits or dresses that look *terrific* in the window don't always look so hotsy-totsy when you see them on *you.* Lots of pins were used, on the backside of the figurine in the window. On you, without the pins, the clothes don't hang quite right, etc., etc.

Likewise, the careers that *sound* terrific in books or in your imagination don't always look so great when you see them up close and personal, in all their living glory.

You need to know that. What you're ultimately trying to find is a career that looks terrific in the window, *and* on you. Toward that end, you are asking what *this* job feels like. There are some questions that will help *(you are talking, of course, with workers who are actually doing the career you think you might like to do):*

- How did you get into this work?
- What do you like the most about it?
- What do you like the least about it?

• And, where else could I find people who do this kind of work? *(You should always ask them for more than one name, so that if you run into a dead end at any point, you can easily go back and visit the other people they suggested.)*

If it becomes apparent to you, during the course of any of these Informational Interviews, that this career, occupation, or job you are exploring definitely *doesn't* fit you, then the last question (above) gets turned into a different kind of inquiry:

• Do you have any ideas as to who else I could go talk to, about my skills and fields of knowledge/interest -- so I can find out how they all might fit together, in one job or career?

Then go visit the people they suggest.

If they can't think of anyone, ask them if they know who *might* know. And so on. And so forth.

"THEY SAY
I HAVE TO GO BACK TO SCHOOL,
BUT I HAVEN'T THE TIME
OR THE MONEY"

Next step: having found the names of jobs or careers that interest you, having mentally *tried them on* to see if they fit, you next want to find out *how much training, etc., it takes, to get into that field or career.* You ask the same people you have been talking to, thus far.

More times than not, you will hear *bad news.* They will tell you something like: "In order to be hired for this job, you have to have a master's degree and ten years' experience at it."

If you're willing to do that, if you have the time, and the money, fine! But what if you don't? Then this is what you do: you search for *the exception:*

"Yes, but do you know of anyone in this field who got into it without that master's degree, and ten years' experience?

And where might I find him or her?

And if you don't know of any such person, who might know some names?"

Throughout your Informational Interviewing, don't assume anything ("But I just assumed that . . ."). Question *all* assumptions, no matter how many people tell you that 'this is the way things are.'

Keep clearly in mind that there are people *out there* who will tell you something that absolutely *isn't* so, with every conviction in their being -- because they *think* it's true. Sincerity they have, one hundred percent. Accuracy is something else again. You will need to check and cross-check any information that people tell you or that you read in books (even this one).

Therefore, no matter how many people tell you that such-and-so are the rules about getting into a particular occupation, and there are no exceptions -- believe me, there *are* exceptions, to almost *every* rule, except where a profession has rigid entrance examinations, as in, say, medicine or law.

Of course rules are rules. But what you are counting on is that somewhere in this vast country, somewhere in this vast world, *somebody* found a way to get into this career you dream of, without going through all the hoops that everyone else is telling you are *absolutely essential.*

You want to find out who these people are, and go talk to them, to find out *how they did it.*

WHEN *SOME* TRAINING
IS UNAVOIDABLE

Okay, but suppose you are determined to go into a career that takes *years* to prepare for; and you can't find *anyone* who took a shortcut? What then?

Even here, you can get *close* to the profession *without* such long preparation. Every professional speciality has one or more *shadow* professions, which require much less training. For example, instead of becoming a doctor, you can go into paramedical work; instead of becoming a lawyer, you can go into paralegal work, etc., etc.

CHOOSE
TWO CAREERS

Anyway, sooner or later, as you interview one person after another, you'll begin to get some definite ideas about a career that is of interest to you. It uses your favorite skills. It employs your favorite fields of knowledge or fields of interest. You've interviewed people *actually doing that work*, and it all sounds fine. This part of your Informational Interviewing is over.

Just be sure that you get the names of at least *two* careers, or jobs, that you think you could be happy doing. Never, ever, put all your eggs in one basket. The secret of surviving out there in the jungle is *having alternatives.*

Be careful. Be thorough. Be persistent. This is your life you're working on, and your future. Make it glorious. Whatever it takes, find out the name of your ideal career, your ideal occupation, your ideal job -- *or jobs.*

Then you are ready to turn to the next two questions:

• QUESTION #2
What **kinds of organizations** would and/or do employ people in these careers?

Before you think of individual places where you might like to work, it is necessary to step back a little, as it were, and think of all the *kinds* of places where one might get hired.

Let's take an example. Suppose in your new career you want to be a teacher. You must then ask yourself: *what kinds of places hire teachers?* You might answer, *"just schools"* -- and finding that schools in your geographical area have no openings, you might say, *"Well, there are no jobs for people in this career."*

But that is not true. There are countless other *kinds* of organizations and agencies out there, besides schools, which employ *teachers.* For example, corporate training and educational departments, workshop sponsors, foundations, private research firms, educational consultants, teachers' associations, professional and trade societies, military bases, state and local councils on higher education, fire and police training academies, and so on, and so forth.

'*Kinds* of places' also means places with different *hiring modes*, besides full-time hiring, such as:

• places that would employ you part-time (maybe you'll end up deciding to hold down two or even three part-time jobs, which altogether would add up to one full-time job, in order to give yourself more variety);

• places that take temporary workers, on assignment for one project at a time;

• places that take consultants, one project at a time;

• places that operate with volunteers, etc.

• places that are nonprofit;

• places that are for profit;

• and, don't forget, places which you yourself would start up, should you decide to be your own boss.

Don't forget that as you talk to workers about their jobs or careers (in the previous section), they will accidentally volunteer information about the *kinds* of organizations. Listen keenly, and keep notes.

• QUESTION #3

Among the kinds of organizations uncovered in the previous question, what are the names of **particular places** that I especially like?

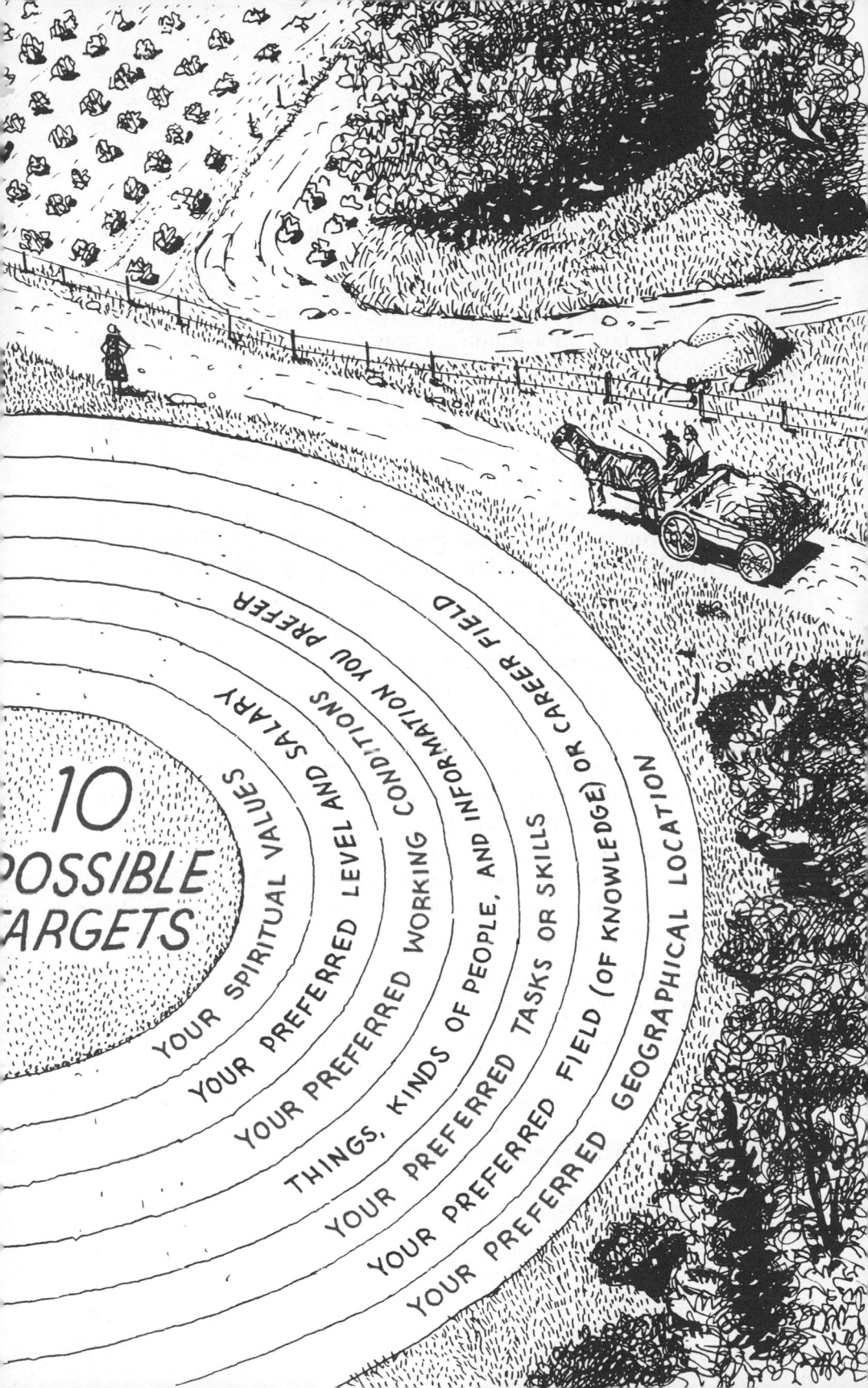

CUTTING DOWN
THE TERRITORY

As you interview workers about their jobs or careers, they will incidentally volunteer actual names of organizations that have such jobs -- including what's good or bad about the place where *they* work. This is important information for you. Jot it all down. Keep notes as though it were part of your religion.

You're going to run into two scenarios: you'll be left with too few names of places to work, or you'll end up with too much information -- too many names of places which hire people in the career that interests you.

We'll take this last scenario, first. If you end up with too many places, you will want to **cut the territory down,** so that you are left with *a manageable number* of 'targets' for your job-hunt.[3]

Let's take an example. Suppose you discovered that the career which interests you the most is *welding.* You want to be a welder. Well, that's a beginning. You've cut the 16 million U.S. job-markets down to:

I want to work in a place that hires welders.

But the territory is still too large. There might be thousands of places in the country, that use welders. You can't go visit them all. So, you've got to cut the territory down, further. Suppose that on your Geography *petal* you said that you really want to live and work in the San Jose area of California. That's helpful: that cuts the territory down further. Now your goal is:

I want to work in a place that hires welders, within the San Jose area.

But, the territory is still too large. There could be 100, 200, 300 organizations which fit that description. So you look at your Flower Diagram for further help, and you notice that under *preferred working conditions* you said you wanted

---

3. If you resist this idea of *cutting the territory down* -- if you feel you could be happy *anywhere* just as long as you were using your favorite skills -- then almost no organization in the country can be ruled out. In the U.S. alone there are currently over 16 million

to work for an organization with fifty or less employees. Good, now your goal is:

> I want to work in a place that hires welders, within the San Jose area, and has fifty or less employees.

This territory may still be too large. So you look again at your Flower Diagram for further guidance, and you see that on the Things *petal* you said you wanted to work for an organization which works with, or produces, *wheels*. So now your statement of what you're looking for, becomes:

> I want to work in a place that hires welders, within the San Jose area, has fifty or less employees, and makes wheels.

Using your Flower Diagram, you can thus keep cutting the territory down, until the *'targets'* of your job-hunt are no more than 10 places. That's a manageable number of places for you to *start with*. You can always expand the list later, if none of these 10 turn out to be very promising or interesting.

EXPANDING THE TERRITORY

Sometimes your problem will be just the opposite. We come here to the second scenario: if your Informational Interviewing doesn't turn up enough names of places where you could get hired in your new career, then you're going to have to consult some directories.

If it's the name of large organizations that you're looking for, see the list on pages *122ff*, in the *Resource Guide*. There are *many* directories of such large organizations.

If it's the name of smaller organizations that you're looking for, your salvation is going to be The Yellow Pages of your local phone book. Look under every related heading that you can think of. Also, see if the Chamber of Commerce publishes a business directory; often it will list not only small companies

---

employers, hence 16 million job-markets, out there. (And a *proportional* number in other countries.) So if you aren't willing to cut the territory down, then you'll have to go visit them all. Good luck! We'll see you in about 43 years.

but also local divisions of larger companies, with names of department heads; and sometimes will even include the (SIC) industry codes. You won't likely lack for names, believe me -- unless it's a very small town you live in, in which case you'll need to cast your net a little wider, to include other towns or villages that are within commuting distance.

Once you have about 10 names of organizations or businesses that might hire you for the kind of work you are dying to do, you proceed to the fourth question:

• QUESTION #4
Among the places that I particularly like, **what needs do they have** or what outcomes are they trying to produce, that my skills and knowledge could help with?

RESEARCHING PLACES
BEFORE YOU APPROACH
THEM

Why should you research places, before you approach them for a hiring-interview? Well, first of all, you want to know something about the organization from the inside: what kind of work they do there. And what their needs or problems or challenges are. And what kind of goals are they trying to achieve, what obstacles are they running into, and how can your skills and knowledges help them? *(When you do at last go in for a hiring-interview, you want above all else to be able to show them that you have something to offer, which they need.)*

Secondly, you want to find out if you would enjoy working there. You want to take the measure of that organization or organizations. Everybody takes the measure of an organization, sooner or later. The problem with most job-hunters or career-changers is they take the measure of an organization *after* they are hired there.

In the U.S., for example, a survey of the Federal/State employment service found that 57% of those who found jobs through that service were not working at that job just 30 days later.

They were not working at that job just thirty days later, *because* they used the first ten or twenty days *on the job* to screen out the job (and some were temorary workers, as well).

By doing this research of a place ahead of time, you are choosing a better way, by far. Essentially, you are *screening out* careers, jobs, places *before* you commit to them. How sensible! How smart!

So, what you do is try to think of every way in the world that you could find out more about those organizations *(plural, not singular)* that interest you, *before you go to see if you can get hired there.* There are several ways you can do this research ahead of time:

• **Friends and Neighbors.** Ask *everybody* you know if they know anyone who works at the place that interests you. And, if they do, ask them if they could arrange for you and that person to get together, for lunch, coffee, or tea. At that time, tell them why the place interests you, and indicate you'd like to know more about it. *(It helps if your mutual friend is sitting there with the two of you, so the purpose of this little chat won't be misconstrued.)* This is the vastly preferred way to find out about a place. However, obviously you need a couple of additional alternatives up your sleeve, in case you run into a dead end here:

• **What's In Print.** The organization itself may have stuff in print, about its business, purpose, etc. The CEO or head of the organization may have given talks. The organization may have copies of those talks. In addition, there may be brochures, annual reports, etc. that the organization has put out, about itself. How do you get ahold of these? The person that answers the phone is the person to check with, in small organizations. In larger organizations, the publicity office, or human relations office, are the places to check. Also, if it's a decent-sized organization that you are interested in, one of the numerous directories mentioned beginning on page *122*, in the *Resource Guide*, may furnish additional information. As well, public libraries may have files on the organization -- newspaper clippings, articles, etc. You never know; and it never hurts to ask your friendly neighborhood research librarian.

• **People at the Organizations in Question, or at Similar Organizations.** You can also go directly to organizations and ask questions about the place, but here I must caution you about several *dangers.*

First, you must make sure you're not asking them questions that are in print somewhere, which you could easily have read for yourself instead of bothering *them.*

Secondly, you must make sure that you approach the people at that organization *whose business it is to give out information* -- receptionists, public relations people, 'the personnel office,' etc., *before* you ever approach other people higher up.

Thirdly, you must make sure that you approach *subordinates* rather than the top person in the place, if the subordinates would know the answer to your questions. Bothering the boss there with some simple questions that someone else could have answered is committing *job-hunting suicide.*

Fourth, you must make sure you're not using this approach simply as a sneaky way to get in to see the boss, and make a pitch for them hiring you. This is information gathering. Keep it at that. Keep it honest.

Job-Hunters Who Are Tricksters

I regret to report that there is no honest, open-hearted job-hunting *technique* that cannot be twisted by those with clever, devious spirits, into some kind of *trick*. This has happened with Informational Interviewing. *Some* job-hunters have thought, "Wouldn't this be a great *trick* to use so as to get in to see employers (not workers) -- asking them for some of their time, claiming you need *information,* and then hitting them up for a job?"

In case *you,* even for a moment, are tempted to follow in their footsteps, let me gently inform you that employers universally detest this particular deception, and have usually thrown the liar/trickster out of their offices.

One New York employer told me what he said to such a trickster: "You came to see me to ask for some information. And I gladly gave you my time. But now, it is apparent you really want a job here, and you think you found a clever 'trick' that would get you in my door. You've essentially lied. Let me tell you something: on the basis of what I have just seen of your style of doing things, I wouldn't hire you if you were the last person on earth."

In this Age of Rudeness, Lies, Manipulation, and Getting Ahead At Any Cost, *you* will want, above all else, to be a beacon of integrity, truth, and kindness throughout your job-hunt or career-change -- including the time you are doing Informational Interviewing. *That's* the kind of employee employers are *dying* to find.

• **Temporary Agencies.** Many job-hunters and career-changers have found that a useful way to explore organizations is to go and work at a temporary agency. Employers turn to these agencies in order to find: a) job-hunters who can work part-time for a limited number of days; and b) job-hunters who can work full-time for a limited number of days. This is an increasing trend. Some companies whose temporary workers comprised only 10% of their total workforce as recently as 1989 are now hiring temps at such a rate that their temporary workers represent from 25 to 60% of their total workforce.[4]

The advantage to you of temporary work is that if there is an agency which loans out people with your particular skills and expertise, you get a chance to visit a number of different employers over a period of several weeks, and see each one from the inside. Maybe temps won't send you to exactly the place you hoped for; but sometimes you can develop contacts over there, even while you're temporarily working somewhere else -- if both organizations are in the same field.

Some of you, of course, may balk at the idea of enrolling with a temporary agency, because you remember the old days when such agencies were solely for clerical workers and secretarial help. But the field has seen an explosion of services in recent years -- according to the Bureau of Labor Statistics, temporary or part-time workers in the U.S. now number over 35 million, and represent 29% of the total civilian labor force.

There are temporary agencies these days *(at least in the larger cities)* for many different occupations. In your city you may find temporary agencies for: accountants, industrial workers, assemblers, drivers, mechanics, construction people, engineering people, software engineers, programmers, computer technicians, production workers, management/executives, nannies (for young and old), health care/dental/medical people, legal specialists, insurance specialists, sales/marketing people, underwriting professionals, financial services, and the like, as well as for the more obvious specialties: data processing, secretarial, and office services. See your local phone book, under 'Temporary Agencies.'

• **Volunteer Work.** Another useful way to research a place before you ever ask them to hire you there, is to volunteer your services at that place that interests you. Of course, some places will turn your offer down, cold. But others will be interested. If they are, it will be relatively easy for you to talk them into letting you work there for a while, because you offer your services *without pay,* and for a brief, limited period of time. In

---

4. *San Francisco Chronicle,* 6/30/94.

other words, from their point of view, if you turn out to be a *pain*, they won't have to endure you for long.

In this fashion, you get a chance to learn about organizations from the inside. Not so coincidentally, if you do decide you would really like to work there, and permanently, they've had a chance to see you in action, and when you are about to end your volunteer time there, *may* want to hire you permanently. I say *may*. Don't be mad if they simply say, "Thanks very much for helping us out." (That's what *usually* happens.) Even so, you've learned a lot, and this will stand you in good stead, in the future -- as you approach other organizations.

SEND A THANK-YOU NOTE

After *anyone* has done you a favor, during this Informational Interviewing phase of your job-hunt, you must *be sure* to send them a thank-you note by the very next day, at the latest. Such a note goes to *everyone* who helps you, or who talks with you. That means friends, people at the organization in question, temporary agency people, secretaries, receptionists, librarians, workers, or whoever.

Ask them, at the time you are face-to-face with them, for their calling card (if they have one), or ask them to write out their name and work-address, on a piece of paper, for you. You *don't* want to misspell their name. It is difficult to figure out how to spell people's names, these days, simply from the sound of it. What sounds like "Laura" may actually be "Lara." What sounds like "Smith" may actually be "Smythe," and so on. Get that name and address, *but get it right,* please. And let me reiterate: write them the thank-you note that same night, or the very next day at the latest. A thank-you note that arrives a week later, completely misses the point.

Ideally it should be handwritten, but if your handwriting is the least bit difficult to read (ranging on up to *indecipherable*), by all means type it. It can be just two or three sentences. Something like: *"I wanted to thank you for talking with me yesterday. It was very helpful to me. I much appreciated your taking the time out of your busy schedule, to do this. Best wishes to you,"* and then your signature. *Do* sign it, particularly if the thank-you note is typed. Typed letters without any signature seem to be multiplying like rabbits in the world of work, these days; the absence of a signature is usually perceived as making your letter *real* impersonal. You don't want to leave that impression.

WHAT IF I GET OFFERED A JOB ALONG THE WAY, WHILE I'M STILL GATHERING ALL THIS INFORMATION?

You probably won't. Let me remind you that during this information gathering, you are *not* talking primarily to employers. You're talking to workers.

Nonetheless, an occasional employer *may* stray across your path during all this Informational Interviewing. And that employer *may* be so impressed with the carefulness you're showing, in going about your career-change and job-search, that they want to hire you, on the spot. So, it's *possible* that you might get offered a job while you're still doing your information gathering. Not *likely,* but *possible.* And if that happens, what should you say?

Well, if you're desperate, you will of course say *yes.* I remember one wintertime when I had just gone through the knee of my last pair of pants, we were burning old pieces of furniture in our fireplace to stay warm, the legs on our bed had just broken, and we were eating spaghetti until it was coming out our ears. In such a situation, *of course* you say yes.

But if you're not *desperate,* if you have a little time to be more careful, then you respond to the job-offer in a way that will buy you some time. You tell them what you're doing: that the average job-hunter tries to screen a job *after* they take it. But you are doing what you are *sure* this employer would do if they were in your shoes: you are examining careers, fields, industries, jobs, organizations *before* you decide where you can do your best and most effective work.

And you tell them that since your Informational Interviewing isn't finished yet, it would be premature for you to accept their job offer, until you're *sure* that this is the place where you could be most effective, and do your best work.

But, you add: "Of course, I'm tickled pink that you would want me to be working here. And when I've finished my personal survey, I'll be glad to get back to you about this, as my preliminary impression is that this is the kind of place I'd like to work in, and the kind of people I'd like to work for, and the kind of people I'd like to work with."

In other words, *if you're not desperate yet,* you don't walk immediately through any opened doors; but neither do you allow them to shut.

A Closing Word to Those Who Are Shy

The late John Crystal[5] had to often counsel the shy. They were often *frightened* at the whole idea of going to talk to people for information, never mind for hiring. So John developed a system to help the shy. He suggested that before you even begin doing any Informational Interviewing, you first go out and talk to people about *anything* just to get good at *talking to people.* Thousands of job-hunters and career-changers have followed his advice, over the past twenty-five years, and found it really helps. Indeed, people who have followed John's advice in this regard have had a success rate of 86% in finding a job --and not just any job, but *the* job or new career that they were looking for.

Daniel Porot, the job-hunting expert in Europe, has taken John's system, and brought some organization to it. He observed that John was really recommending three types of interviews: this interview we are talking about, just for practice. Then Informational Interviewing. And finally, of course, the hiring-interview. Daniel decided to call these three the *'The PIE Method,'* which has helped thousands of job-hunters and career-changers in both the U.S. and in Europe. Porot's "PIE Chart" follows on the next page:

---

5. John also was the inventor of WHAT, WHERE, and HOW -- which I have used as the basic framework for Chapters 5, 6, and 7, here.

Initial:	Pleasure **P**	Information **I**	Employment **E**
Kind of Interview	Practice Field Survey	Informational Interviewing or Researching	Employment Interview or Hiring Interview
Purpose	To Get Used to Talking with People to Enjoy It; To "Penetrate" Networks	To Find Out If You'd Like a Job, Before You Go Trying to Get It	To Get Hired for the Work You Have Decided You Would Most Like to Do
How You Go to the Interview	You Can Take Somebody with You	By Yourself or You Can Take Somebody with You	By Yourself
Who You Talk To	Anyone Who Shares Your Enthusiasm About a (for You) Non-Job-Related Subject	A Worker Who Is Doing the Actual Work You Are Thinking About Doing	An Employer Who Has the Power to Hire You for the Job You Have Decided You Would Most Like to Do
How Long a Time You Ask For	10 Minutes (and DON'T run over -- asking to see them at 11:50 may help keep you honest, since most employers have lunch appoint-ments at noon)	Ditto	
What You Ask Them	Any Curiosity You Have About Your Shared Interest or Enthusiasm	Any Questions You Have About This Job or This Kind of Work	You Tell Them What It Is You Like About Their Organization and What Kind of Work You Are Looking For.

Initial:	Pleasure **P**	Information **I**	Employment **E**
What You Ask Them *(continued)*	If Nothing Occurs to You, Ask: 1. How did you start, with this hobby, interest, etc.? 2. What excites or interests you the most about it? 3. What do you find is the thing you like the least about it? 4. Who else do you know of who shares this interest, hobby or enthusiasm, or could tell me more about my curiosity? a. Can I go and see them? b. May I mention that it was you who suggested I see them? c. May I say that you recommended them? ***Get their name and address***	If Nothing Occurs to You, Ask: 1. How did you get interested in this work and how did you get hired? 2. What excites or interests you the most about it? 3. What do you find is the thing you like the least about it? 4. Who else do you know of who does this kind of work, or similar work but with this difference: _____? 5. What kinds of challenges or problems do you have to deal with in this job? 6. What skills do you need in order to meet those challenges or problems? ***Get their name and address***	 You tell them the kinds of challenges you like to deal with. What skills you have to deal with those challenges. What experience you have had in dealing with those challenges in the past.
AFTERWARD: That Same Night	SEND A THANK YOU NOTE	SEND A THANK YOU NOTE	SEND A THANK YOU NOTE

Why is it called *'PIE'*? [6]

P is for the *warmup* phase. John Crystal named this warmup 'The Practice Field Survey.'[7] Daniel Porot calls it **P** for *pleasure.*

I is for 'Informational Interviewing.'

E is for the employment interview with the-person-who-has-the-power-to-hire-you.

How do you use this **P** for *practice* to get comfortable about going out and talking to people *one-on-one*?

This is achieved by choosing a topic -- *any* topic, however silly or trivial -- that is a pleasure for you to talk about with your friends, or family. To avoid anxiety, it should not be a topic that is connected to any present or future career that you are considering. Rather, the kinds of topics that work best, for this exercise, are:

• **a hobby** you *love*, such as skiing, bridge playing, exercise, computers, etc.

• **any leisure-time enthusiasm** of yours, such as a movie you just saw, that you liked a lot

• **a long-time curiosity**, such as how do they predict the weather, or what do policemen do

• **an aspect of the town or city you live in**, such as a new shopping mall that just opened

• **an issue** you feel strongly about, such as the homeless, AIDS sufferers, ecology, peace, health, etc.

There is only one condition about choosing a topic: it should be something you *love* to talk about with other people: a subject you know nothing about, but you feel a great deal of enthusiasm for it, is far preferable to something you know an awful lot about, but it puts you to sleep.

---

6. Daniel has summarized his system in a new book published here in the U.S.: it is called *The PIE Method for Career Success: A Unique Way to Find Your Ideal Job*, 1996, and is available from its publisher, JIST Works, Inc., 720 North Park Avenue, Indianapolis IN 46202-3431. Phone 317-264-3720. Fax 317-264-3709. It is a fantastic book, and I give it my highest recommendation.

7. If you want further instructions about this whole process, I refer you to "The Practice Field Survey," pp. 187–196 in *Where Do I Go From Here With My Life?* by John Crystal and friend. Ten Speed Press, Box 7123, Berkeley, CA 94707.

Enthusiasm

Throughout the job-hunt and career-change, the key to 'interviewing' is not found in memorizing a dozen rules about what you're supposed to say.

No, the key is just this one thing: now and always, be *sure* you are talking about something you feel *passionate about.*[8]

Enthusiasm is the key -- to *enjoying* 'interviewing,' and conducting *effective* interviews, at any level. What this **P** exercise teaches us is that shyness always loses its power and its painful self-consciousness -- *if* and *when* you are talking about something *you love.*

For example, if you love gardens you will forget all about your shyness when you're talking to someone else about gardens and flowers. *"You ever been to Butchart Gardens?"*

If you love movies, you'll forget all about your shyness when you're talking to someone else about movies. *"I just hated that scene where they . . ."*

If you love computers, then you will forget all about your shyness when you're talking to someone else about computers. *"Do you work on a Mac or an MS-DOS machine?*

That's why it is important that it be your enthusiasms -- here, your hobbies -- later, in Informational Interviewing, your *favorite* skills and your *favorite* subjects -- that you are exploring and pursuing in these conversations with others.

Having identified your enthusiasm, you then need to go talk to someone who is as enthusiastic about this thing, as you are. *For best results with your later job-hunt, this should be someone you don't already know.* Use the Yellow Pages, ask around among your friends and family, *who do you know that loves to talk about this?* It's relatively easy to find the kind of person you're looking for.

You love to talk about skiing? *Try a ski-clothes store, or a skiing instructor.* You love to talk about writing? *Try a professor on a nearby college campus, who teaches English.* You love to talk about physical exercise? *Try a trainer, or someone who teaches physical therapy.*

Once you've identified someone you think shares your enthusiasm, you then go talk with them. When you are face-to-face with your *fellow enthusiast,* the first thing you must do is relieve their understandable anxiety. *Everyone* has had someone visit them who has stayed too long, who has worn out their welcome. If your *fellow enthusiast* is worried about you staying too long, they'll be so preoccupied with this that they won't hear a word you are saying.

So, when you first meet them, ask for *ten minutes of their time, only.* Period. Stop. Exclamation point. And watch your wristwatch *like a hawk,* to be sure

---

8. This is what the late Joseph Campbell used to call 'your bliss.'

you stay no longer. *Never* stay longer, unless they *beg* you to. And I mean, *beg, beg, beg.*[9]

Once they've agreed to give you ten minutes, you tell them why you're there -- that you're trying to get comfortable about talking with people, for information -- and you understand that you two share a mutual interest, which is . . .

Then what? Well, a topic may have its own unique set of questions. For example, I love movies, so if I met someone who shared this interest, my first question would be, "What movies have you seen lately?" And so on. If it's a topic you love, and often talk about, you'll *know* what kinds of questions you begin with. But, if no such questions come to mind, no matter how hard you try, the following ones have proved to be good conversation starters for thousands of job-hunters and career-changers before you, no matter what their topic or interest.

So, look these over, memorize them *(or copy them on a little card that fits in the palm of your hand),* and give them a try:

Questions Shy People Can Practice With

Addressed to the person you're doing the Practice Interviewing with:

- How did you get involved with/become interested in this? ("*This*" is the hobby, curiosity, aspect, issue, or enthusiasm, that you are so interested in.)
- What do you like the most about it?
- What do you like the least about it?
- Who else would you suggest I go talk to that shares this interest?
- Can I use your name?
- May I tell them it was you who recommended that I talk with them?
- *Then, choosing one person off the list of several names they may have given you, you say,* Well, I think I will begin by going to talk to this person. Would you be willing to call ahead for me, so they will know who I am, when I go over there?

---

9. A polite, "Oh do you have to go?" should be understood for what it is: politeness. Your response should be, "Yes, I promised to only take ten minutes of your time, and I want to keep to my word." This will almost always leave a *very* favorable impression behind you.

Incidentally, during *this* Practice Interviewing, it's perfectly okay for you to take someone with you -- preferably someone who is more outgoing than you feel you are. And on the first few interviews, let them take the lead in the conversation, while you watch to see how they do it.

Once it is *your turn* to conduct the interview, it will by that time usually be easy for you to figure out what to talk about.

Alone or with someone, keep at this Practice Interviewing until you feel very much at ease in talking with people and asking them questions about things you are curious about.

In all of this, *fun* is the key. If you're having fun, you're doing it right. If you're not having fun, you need to keep at it, until you are. It may take your seeing four people. It may take ten. Or twenty. You'll know.

Summary of This Chapter

There is no limit to what you can find out about **WHERE** you'd like to work -- careers, and places which hire for those careers -- if you go out and talk to people. When you find places that interest you, it is irrelevant whether they happen to have a vacancy, or not. In this dance of life, called the job-hunt, you get to decide first of all whether or not *you* want *them*, through your research. Only after you have decided that, is it appropriate to ask, as in the next chapter, if they also want you.

---

*You're a bunch of jackasses. You work your
rear ends off in a trivial course that no one
will ever care about again. You're not willing
to spend time researching a company that
you're interested in working for. Why don't
you decide who you want to work for and
go after them?*

Professor Albert Shapiro,
*The late William H. Davis Professor
of The American Free Enterprise System
at Ohio State University*

FOR
THE DETERMINED
JOB-HUNTER
OR
CAREER-CHANGER

The Systematic Approach To
Career-Change
And Job-Hunting

HOW

DO YOU OBTAIN SUCH A JOB?

You Must Identify The Person Who Has The Power to
Hire You, and Show Them How Your Skills Can Help
Them With Their Problems

Chapter 7

Table of Contents

How
To Get A Hiring Interview

Okay, so you've identified a job you love, you've found a place -- better yet, *places* -- where you'd *love* to work. But . . .

But, the person you'd have to see, in order to get hired there, is in an office with a ring of fire around it, three knights in full armor guarding it, in a castle with fifty-foot walls, surrounded by a wide moat whose deep waters are filled with hungry alligators.

And you want to know how to get a hiring-interview with this person. Right? Well, it isn't as difficult as it might at first seem . . . if you are *determined*. And if you know a few simple principles.

THE FIRST CRUCIAL QUESTION: HOW LARGE IS THE ORGANIZATION?

To begin with, most discussions of job-interviewing proceed from a false assumption. That is, they *assume* you are going to be approaching a large organization -- you know, the ones where you need a floor-plan of the building, and an alphabetical directory of the staff.

There are admittedly *huge* problems in approaching such giants for a hiring-interview, not the least of which is that many are doing more downsizing than hiring, during these cost-cutting times.[1]

But many job-hunters don't want to work for large corporations, anyway. They want to go after the so-called 'small organizations' -- those with 50 or less employees -- which, in the U.S., for example, total 80% of all private businesses, and represent one-fourth of all workers in the private sector.

These small organizations create -- experts say -- two-thirds, or more, of all new jobs.[2] Which is a good thing, because small organizations are *much* easier to get into than large ones, believe me.

With a small organization, you don't need to wait until there's a *known* vacancy, because they rarely advertise vacancies

---

1. Like all generalizations, this one of course has a number of exceptions. In the U.S., Wal-Mart, Pepsico, U.P.S., Chrysler, Sara Lee, General Mills, Motorola, and Home Depot all added jobs -- in Wal-Mart's case, 182,000 -- between 1992 and 1994. Wal-Mart thus became the second largest employer in the U.S. *(New York Times, 3/25/94).*

2. This statistic, first popularized by David Birch of M.I.T., and 'bandied about' for years, has been widely debated, during the '90s, by economists such as Nobel laureate Milton Friedman and Harvard economist James Medoff. The debate has been fueled by a study conducted jointly by Steven J. Davis, a labor economist at the University of Chicago, John Haltiwanger at the University of Maryland, and Scott Schuh at the Federal Reserve. Their study, however, was of U.S. *manufacturing*, not of the economy as a whole. Anyway, picky-smicky, what these researchers discovered is that small *manufacturing* companies with 50 or fewer employees created only *one-fifth* of all new manufacturing jobs. *(New York Times, 3/25/94).* Other researchers, such as Birch, had attributed a much larger percentage to small companies. Here and elsewhere, critics often concede that small companies do create a lot of the new jobs in the *overall economy*, but then *sniff*, "Small businesses are not the places you see *the best* jobs," as one economist put it. (The emphasis is mine.) 'Best jobs' mean -- to these critics -- jobs with high pay, high benefits, government-mandated health and safety regulations, and union representation. *(San Francisco Chronicle, 3/29/93).*

even when there is one. You just go there and ask if they need someone.

With a small organization, there is no Personnel or Human Resources Department to screen you out.

With a small organization, there's no problem in identifying the person-who-has-the-power-to-hire-you. It's *the boss*. Everyone there knows who it is. They can point to his or her office door, easily.

With a small organization, you do not need to approach them through the mail; you can go in to see the boss. And if, by chance, he or she is well-protected from intruders, it is relatively easy to figure out how to get around *that*. Contacts are the answer, as we shall see.

With a small organization, if it is growing, there is a greater likelihood that they will be willing to create a new position for you, *if you quietly convince them that you are too good to let slip out of their grasp*.

For all of these reasons and more, small organizations must be kept in mind, as much as large organizations, when we begin talking about techniques or strategies for securing a hiring-interview. And, we therefore need to talk about two different techniques:

How you approach a large organization.

And, how you approach a small organization.

Two different approaches, altogether.

APPROACHING
LARGE ORGANIZATIONS
FOR AN INTERVIEW

In securing hiring-interviews, it's the large organizations that are the problem -- the ones, as I mentioned before, where you need a floor-plan of the building, and an alphabetical directory of the staff.

But we can simplify our task, if we keep certain things in mind. To begin with, you don't want to just get into the building. You want to see *a particular person* in that building, and only that person: namely, the person-who-has-the-power-to-hire-you for the job you are interested in.

Most job-hunters *don't* even *try* to find out *who* that person is, before approaching a large organization. Rather, they approach each large organization in what can only be described as a haphazard, scatter-shot fashion -- sending them their resume or c.v.[3] -- with or without some covering letter -- hoping

3. C.v. stands for *curriculum vitae*, a term for *resume* that is favored in academic circles in the U.S. and in other countries.

that resume or covering letter will function as a kind of extended calling-card, arousing employers' interest, so they will ask the job-hunter to come in and see them.

This is many job-hunters' favorite way of approaching an organization, particularly a large organization, for a hiring-interview. It's their favorite because you don't have to *go* somewhere needlessly, you don't have to look into the employers' eyes when they reject you, and -- let's admit it, sometimes it actually works: you do get invited in for a possible hiring-interview.

On the other hand, *some* employers also love this 'mail approach,' but for very different reasons. They love it, because it enables them to screen you out *in about eight seconds,* without ever 'wasting their time' on your coming in for an interview.

It is therefore *very common* for job-hunters to approach eight hundred organizations or more in this fashion and not get *one* single invitation to come in for a hiring-interview. You, of course, falsely thinking this is a method that works well for *most* job-hunters, will wonder what is wrong with you; you not only don't find a job this way, but you end up with much-lowered self-esteem. If you try this approach and it doesn't work, don't feel there is something wrong with you. There's something wrong with this method!!

It goes without saying that there are certain situations where you may *want* to have a resume -- for example, if you're talking to some employer who is halfway across the country, or if you're having a *series* of interviews with some particular place locally, and you want to *leave* a resume behind you, *after* the first interview, for the interviewing officer to share with those there who haven't met you yet.

The most important rule about preparing your resume or c.v. is that there is no such thing as a *right* format or form for a resume or c.v. I used to have a hobby of collecting 'winning' resumes -- that is, resumes that had actually gotten someone a hiring-interview and, ultimately, a job. Being playful by nature, I delighted in showing these, without comment, to employers whom I knew. Many of them didn't like the winning resumes at all. "That resume will never get anyone a job," they would say.

Then, I would tell them, "Sorry, you're wrong. It already has. What you are saying is that it wouldn't get them a job *with you.*"

The resume reproduced on the next page is a good example of what I mean. (*You did want an example of what I mean, didn't you?*) Jim Dyer, who had been in the Marines for twenty years, wanted a job as a salesman for heavy construction and mining equipment thousands of miles from where he was then living. He devised the resume you see, and had fifteen copies made. "I used," he said, "a grand total of seven before I got the job in the place I wanted!"

Like the employer who hired him, I loved this resume. Yet, other employers have criticized it for using a picture, for being too long (or too short), etc., etc. In other words, had Jim sent his resume to *them,* they wouldn't have been impressed enough to invite him in for an interview. So, don't believe anyone who tells you there's one right format for a resume, or one style that's guaranteed to win. After four thousand years, we've still gotten no further than the *ink-blot* stage in hiring, where one thing means something to one employer, but something quite different to another. So, when you mail it out, basically what you're doing is hoping and praying that this resume of yours will appeal to *those employers who appeal to you.*

There are always going to be millions of employers who don't like resumes in general, or don't like *your* resume in particular. Some employers are so highly allergic to resumes -- period -- that they break out into a rash, if they see even one in their mail. Hence, oftentimes a brief individual letter, summarizing the same stuff, is preferable to sending someone your resume.

There is a far far more effective way to approach employers -- and that is to identify *who* at that organization has the power to hire you for the position you have in mind, and then to discover what mutual friend the two of you might have in common, who could help you get an appointment. **The person-who-has-the-power-to-hire-you** will see you because of that mutual friend having gotten the appointment for you.

It is astonishing how often this approach works -- it has, in fact, an 86% effectiveness rate for getting a hiring-interview and, subsequently, a job.

E.J. DYER   Street, City, Zip   Telephone No.

I SPEAK
THE LANGUAGE
OF
MEN
MACHINERY
AND
MANAGEMENT
. . .

OBJECTIVE: Sales of Heavy Equipment

QUALIFICATIONS   * Knowledge of heavy equipment, its use and maintenance.

* Ability to communicate with management and with men in the field.

* Ability to favorably introduce change in the form of new equipment or new ideas... the ability to sell.

EXPERIENCE   * Maintained, shipped, budgeted and set allocation priorities for 85 pieces of heavy equipment as head of a 500-man organization
Men and   (1975-1977).
Machinery

* Constructed twelve field operation support complexes, employing a 100-man crew and 19 pieces of heavy equipment (1965-1967).

* Jack-hammer operator, heavy construction (summers 1956-1957-1958).

Management   * Planned, negotiated and executed large scale equipment purchases on a nation to nation level (1972-1974).

Sales   * Achieved field customer acceptance of two major new computer-based systems:
  - Equipment inventory control and repair parts expedite system (1968-1971)
  - Decision makers' training system (1977-1979).
* Proven leader ... repeatedly elected or appointed to senior posts.

EDUCATION   * B.A. Benedictine College, 1959. (Class President; Editor Yearbook; "Who's Who in American Colleges").

* Naval War College, 1975. (Class President; Graduated "With Highest Distinction").

* University of Maryland, 1973-1974. (Chinese Language).

* Middle Level Management Training Course, 1967-1968 (Class Standing: 1 of 97).

PERSONAL   * Family: Sharon and our sons Jim (11), Andy (8) and Matt (5) desire to locate in a Mountain State by 1982, however, in the interim will consider a position elsewhere in or outside the United States ... Health: Excellent ... Birthdate: December 9, 1937 ... Completing Military Service with the rank of Lieutenant Colonel, U.S. Marine Corps.

SUMMARY   A seeker of challenge ... experienced, proven and confident of closing the sales for profit.

Of course, there is that 14% of the time when it *doesn't* work. There are places where it is absolutely *impossible* to get in to see 'the boss,' i.e., the one who has the power to hire you, in spite of *contacts*, mutual friends, or whatever. As mentioned earlier, he or she may be isolated in a castle surrounded by a moat, with eight large, oversized, hungry alligators in that moat. You of course will hurl yourself against the ramparts of that castle a half-dozen times, anyway, furious that you can't get in to see that person, despite all the techniques recommended in this book.

But, could I ask you a question: "*Why* do you want to work for *a place like that*?" I mean, never mind that you're understandably taking this very personally. *Rejection, rejection, rejection,* is flashing on and off in your brain. But, haven't they *(by these actions)* told you something about *the way they work* that is important information for you to have? And having gained that information, isn't it time for you to reassess *whether you really want to work at a place so guarded, so impenetrable, so 'un-user-friendly'*?

How
To Use Your Contacts
To Get That Interview

HOW DO I FIND OUT
EXACTLY WHO HAS THE POWER
TO HIRE ME?

In a small organization with 50 or less employees, this is a relatively easy problem. Calling the place and asking for the name of the boss, should do it. It's what we call *The One-Minute Research Project.*

But if the place where you are dying to work is a much larger organization, then the answer is: "Through the *research* you already learned how to do in Chapter 6; *and* by asking every *contact* you have."

Let's say the one of the places you are interested in is an organization which we will call *Mythical Corporation.*

You know the kind of job you'd like to get there, but first you know you need to find out the name of **the person-who-has-the-power-to-hire-you** there. What do you do?

If it's a large organization, you go on the Internet or you go to your local public library, and search the directories there. I have listed these on pages *122* and *161*. Hopefully that search will yield the name of the person you want.

But if it doesn't, which will particularly be the case with smaller organizations, *then you turn to your contacts.*

Who or What Is "A Contact"?

Since this subject of *contacts* is widely misunderstood by job-hunters and career-changers, let's be very specific, here.

Every person you know, is a contact.

Every member of your family.

Every friend of yours.

Every person in your address book.

Every person on your Christmas-card list.

Every merchant or salesperson you ever deal with.

Every person who comes to your apartment or house to do any kind of repairs or maintenance work.

Every check-out clerk you know.

Every gas station attendant you know.

Every leisure partner you have, as for walking, exercising, swimming, or whatever.

Every doctor, or medical professional you know.

Every professor, teacher, etc., you once knew or maybe still know how to get ahold of.

Every clergyperson, rabbi, or religious leader you know.

Every person in your church, synagogue, mosque, or religious assembly.

Everyone you know in Rotary, Kiwanis, Lions, or other service organizations.

Every person you are newly introduced to.

Every person you meet, stumble across, or blunder into, during your job-hunt, whose name, address, and phone number you have the grace to ask for. (*Always* have the grace to ask for it.)

Got the picture?

So now, to our task. You approach as many people as necessary, among all those you know, and you ask each of them, "Do you know anyone who works, or used to work, at *Mythical Corporation?*"

You ask that question again and again of *everyone* you know, or meet, until you find someone who says, "*Yes, I do.*"

Then you ask them:

• "What is the name of the person you know who works, or used to work, at *Mythical Corporation?* Do you have their phone number and/or address?"

• "Would you be willing to call ahead, to tell them who I am?"

• You then either phone them yourself or make an appointment to go see them ("*I won't need more than 10 minutes of your time.*") Once you are talking to them, after the usual polite chit-chat, you ask them the question you are dying to know. Because they are *inside* the organization that interests you, they are usually able to give you the exact answer to the question that has been puzzling you: "Who would have the power to hire me at *Mythical Corporation,* for this kind of position *(which you then describe)?*" If they answer that they do not know, ask if they know *who* might know. If it turns out that they do know, then you ask them not only for that hiring person's name, address, phone, and e-mail address, but also what they can tell you about that person's job, that person's interests, and their style of interviewing.

• Then, you ask them if they could help you get an appointment with that person. You repeat once again the familiar refrain:

• "Given my background, would you recommend I go see them?"

• "Do you know them, personally? If not, could you give me the name of someone who does?"

• "If you know them personally, may I tell them it was you who recommended that I talk with them?"

• "If you know them personally, would you be willing to call ahead, to tell them who I am, and to help set up an appointment?"

Also, before leaving, you can also ask them about the organization, in general.

Then you thank them, and leave; and you *never never* let the day end, without sitting down to write them a thank-you note. *Always* do it. *Never* forget to.

RESCUING THE EMPLOYER

As you can see, getting in to see someone, even for a hiring-interview, is not all that difficult. Everyone has friends, including this **person-who-has-the-power-to-hire-you**. You are simply approaching them through *their* friends. And you are doing this, not *wimpishly,* as one who is coming to ask a favor. You are doing it *helpfully,* as one who is asking to help rescue them.

Rescue? Yes, rescue! I cannot tell you the number of employers I have known over the years, who can't figure out how to find the right employee. It is absolutely mind-boggling, particularly in these hard times when job-hunters would seem to be gathered on every street corner.

You're having trouble finding the employer. The employer is having trouble finding you. *What a great country!*

So, if you now present yourself directly to **the person-who-has-the-power-to-hire-you**, you are not only answering your own prayers. You are hopefully answering the employer's, as well. You will be *just* what the employer is looking for, but didn't know how to find, if . . .

if you took the trouble to do Chapters 5 and 6, and

if you took the trouble to figure out what are your favorite and best skills, and

if you took the trouble to figure out what are your favorite and best subjects or *languages*, and

if you took the trouble to figure out what places *might* need such skills and such *languages*, and

if you researched this place with the intent of finding out what their tasks, challenges, and problems are, and

if you took the trouble to figure out who there has the power to hire you.

Of course, you don't for sure *know* they need you; that remains for the hiring-interview to uncover. But at least by this thorough preparation you have *increased* the chances that you are at the right place -- whether they have an announced vacancy or not. And, if you are, you are not imposing on this employer. You are coming not as 'job-beggar,' but as 'resource person.' You may well be rescuing him or her, believe me.

MAY-DAY, MAY-DAY!

Whenever a job-hunter writes me and tells me they've run into a brick wall, and just can't find out the name of **the person-who-has-the-power-to-hire-them**, the problem *always* turns out to be: they aren't making *sufficient* use of their contacts. They're making a *pass* at using their contacts, but they aren't putting their whole heart and soul into it.

My favorite (true) story in this regard, concerns a job-hunter I know, in Virginia. He decided he wanted to work for a particular health-care organization in that State, and not knowing any better, he approached them by visiting their Human Resources Department. After dutifully filling out a job application, and talking to someone there in that department, he was told there were no jobs available. Stop. Period. End of story.

Approximately three months later he learned about this technique of approaching your favorite organization by using contacts. He explored his contacts *diligently*, and succeeded in getting an interview with the person-who-had-the-power-to-hire-him for the position he was interested in. The two of them hit it off, immediately. The appointment went swimmingly. "You're hired," said the person-who-had-the-power-to-hire-him. "I'll call Human Resources and tell them you're hired, and that you'll be down to fill out the necessary stuff."

Our job-hunter never once mentioned that he had previously approached that same organization through that same Human Resources Department, and been turned down cold.

Just remember: contacts are the key. It takes about eighty pairs of eyes, and ears, to help find the career, the workplace, the job that you are looking for.

Your contacts *are* those eyes and ears.

They are what will help you get the ideal job you are looking for, and they are key to finding out the name of the person-who-has-the-power-to-hire-you.

The more people you know, the more people you meet, the more people you talk to, the more people you enlist as part of your own personal job-hunting network, the better your job-finding success is likely to be.

Some job-hunters cultivate new contacts wherever they go, during their time of unemployment. For example, if they go to hear a speaker on some subject that interests them, they make it a point to join the crowd that gathers 'round the speaker at the end of the talk, and -- with notepad poised -- ask such questions as: "Is there anything special that people with my expertise can do?" And here they mention their *generalized* job-title: computer scientist, health professional, chemist, writer, or whatever. Very useful information has thus been turned up. You can also go up to the speaker afterwards, and ask if you can contact him or her for further information -- "and at what address?"

Conventions, likewise, afford rich opportunities to make contacts. Says one college graduate: "I snuck into the Cable Advertisers Convention at the Waldorf in N.Y.C. That's how I got my job."

Another way people have cultivated contacts, is to leave a message on their telephone answering machine which tells

everyone who calls, what information they are looking for. One job-hunter used the following message: "This is the recently laid off John Smith. I'm not home right now because I'm out looking for a good job as a computer trouble-shooter in the telecommunications field; if you have any leads or just want to leave a message, please leave it after the tone."

You may also cultivate contacts by studying the *things* that you like to work with, and then writing to the manufacturer of that *thing* to ask them for a list of organizations in your geographical area which use that *thing*. For example, if you like to work on a particular machine, you would write to the manufacturer of that machine, and ask for names of organizations in your geographical area which use that machine. Or if you like to work in a particular environment, think of the supplies used in that environment. For example, let's say you love darkrooms. You think of what brand equipment or supplies is usually used in darkrooms, and then you contact the sales manager of the company that makes those supplies, to ask where his (or her) customers are. Some sales managers will not be at all responsive to such an inquiry; but others graciously will, and thus you may gain some very helpful leads.

Because your memory is going to be overloaded during your job-hunt or career-change, it is useful to set up a filing system, where you put the name of each contact of yours on a 3×5 card, with addresses, phone numbers, and anything about where they work or who they know that may be of use at a later date. Go back over those cards frequently.

That does add up to *a lot* of file cards, just because you've got *a lot* of contacts. But that's the whole point.

You may need *every one* of them, *when push comes to shove*.

GETTING IN

If the contact you talked to, doesn't know **the person-who-has-the-power-to-hire-you** well enough to get you an interview, then you go back to your other contacts -- now armed with the name of the person you are trying to get in to see -- and pose a new question. Approaching as many of your contacts as necessary, you ask each of them, "Do you know Ms. or Mr. See, at *Mythical Corporation* or do you know someone who does?"

You ask that question again and again of *everyone* who is on your file cards, until you find someone who says, *"Yes, I do."*

Then of course, over the phone or -- better -- in person, you ask them the same familiar questions, carefully, and in this exact order:

- "What can you tell me about him -- or her?"
- "Given the kind of job I am looking for *(which you here describe)*, do you think it would be worth my while to go see them?"
- "Do you have their phone number and/or address?"
- "May I tell them it was you who recommended that I talk with them?"
- "Would you be willing to call ahead, to set up an appointment for me, and tell them who I am?"

When you've gotten an appointment, in this fashion, *that* is the time of course that you will begin to sweat. *"The hiring-interview! I'm actually there."*

THE TEN GREATEST MISTAKES MADE IN JOB INTERVIEWS

Whereby Your Chances of Finding a Job Are Greatly Decreased

I. Going after large organizations only (such as the Fortune 500).

II. Hunting all by yourself for places to visit, using ads and resumes.

III. Doing no homework on an organization before going there.

IV. Allowing the Personnel Department (or Human Resources) to interview you -- *their primary function is to screen you OUT.*

V. Setting no time limit when you make the appointment with an organization.

VI. Letting your resume be used as the agenda for the job interview.

VII. Talking primarily about yourself, and what benefit the job will be for you.

VIII. When answering a question of theirs, talking anywhere from 2 to 15 minutes, at a time.

IX. Basically approaching them as if you were a job-beggar, hoping they will offer you a job, however humble.

X. Not sending a thank-you note right after the interview.

THE TEN COMMANDMENTS
FOR JOB INTERVIEWS

Whereby Your Chances of Finding a Job Are Vastly Increased

I. Go after small organizations, with twenty or less employees, since they create 2/3 of all new jobs.

II. Hunt for interviews using the aid of friends and acquaintances, because a job-hunt requires fifty eyes and ears.

III. Do thorough homework on an organization before going there, using Informational Interviews plus the library.

IV. At any organization, identify who has the power to hire you there, for the position you want, and use your friends and acquaintances' contacts, to get in to see that person.

V. Ask for just 20 minutes of their time, when asking for the appointment; and keep to your word.

VI. Go to the interview with your own agenda, your own questions and curiosities about whether or not this job fits you.

VII. Talk about yourself only if what you say offers some benefit to that organization, and their 'problems.'

VIII. When answering a question of theirs, talk only between 20 seconds and 2 minutes, at any one time.

IX. Basically approach them as if you were a resource person, able to produce better work for that organization than any predecessor.

X. Always write a thank-you note the same evening of the interview, and mail it at the latest by the next morning.

How

To Conduct An Interview

Yes, you're there. But do not be afraid as you go to meet the person-who-has-the-power-to-hire-you. There are several comforting thoughts you may cling to.

FIRST COMFORTING THOUGHT: IN A HIRING-INTERVIEW, YOU'RE STILL DOING RESEARCH

Your natural question, as you approach any job-interview, tends to be, "How do I convince this employer to hire me?" Wrong question. It implies that you have already made up your mind that this would be a grand place to work at, and a grand person to work for, so that all that remains is for you to sell yourself. This is rarely the case. In most cases, despite your best attempts to research the place thoroughly, you don't know enough about it yet, to say that. You have *got* to use the hiring-interview as a chance to gather further information about this organization, and this boss.

If you understand *this* about an interview, you will be ahead of 98% of all other job-hunters -- who all too often go to the hiring-interview as a lamb goes to the slaughter, or as a criminal goes on trial before a judge.

You *are* on trial, of course, in the employer's eyes.

But, so is that employer and that organization, in *your* eyes.

This is what makes the job interview tolerable or even enjoyable: you are studying everything about this employer, at the same time that they are studying everything about you.

Two people, both sizing each other up. You know what that reminds you of. Dating, of course. Well, the job interview is every bit like 'the dating game.' Both of you have to like each other, before you can even discuss the question of *'going steady,'* i.e., a job. So, you're sitting there, sizing each other up. *Great!*

The importance of your doing your own weighing of this person, this organization, and this job, *during* the hiring-interview, cannot be overstated. The tradition in the U.S., and throughout the world for that matter, is to find a job, take it, and *then* try to figure out in the next three months, after you're in it, whether it is a good job or not -- quitting if you decide it isn't.

You are going against that stupid tradition, as any sensible job-hunter or career-changer should, by using the hiring-interview to screen the organization *before you go to work there* -- saving yourself grief, guilt, and lost time.

For thus, in effect, *quitting before you're offered the job,* rather than *quitting after you've taken the job,* the employer will thank you, your Mother will thank you, your spouse or partner will thank you, and of course you yourself will thank you.

"I'm hoping to find something in a meaningful, humanist, outreach kind of bag, with flexible hours, non-sexist bosses, and fabulous fringes."

SECOND COMFORTING THOUGHT: HIRING-INTERVIEWS ARE NOT A SCIENCE

As you go to the interview, do remember that **the person-who-has-the-power-to-hire-you** is sweating too. Why? Because, the hiring-interview is not a very reliable way to choose an employee. In a survey conducted among a dozen top United Kingdom employers,[4] it was discovered that the chances of an employer finding a good employee through the hiring interview was only *3% better* than if they had picked a name out of a hat. In a further ironic finding, it was discovered that if the interview were conducted by someone who would be working directly with the candidate, the success rate dropped to *2% below* that of picking a name out of a hat. And if the interview were conducted by a so-called personnel expert, the success rate dropped to *10% below* that of picking a name out of a hat.

No, I don't know how they came up with these figures. But they are totally consistent with what I know of the world of hiring. I have watched so-called personnel or human resources experts make *wretchedly* bad choices about hiring in their own office, and when they would morosely confess this to me some months later, over lunch, I would tease them with, "If you don't even know how to hire well, yourselves, how do you keep a straight face when you're called in as consultant by another organization?" And they would ruefully reply, "We treat it *as though it were* a science."

Well, let me tell you, dear reader, the hiring-interview is *not* a science. It is a very very hazy art, and done badly by most of its employer-practitioners, in spite of their good heart, their very best intentions, and their carloads of goodwill.

---

4. Reported in the *Financial Times Career Guide 1989* in the United Kingdom.

THIRD COMFORTING THOUGHT:
OFTENTIMES THE EMPLOYER IS
AS SCARED AS YOU ARE

So, you are sitting there with sweaty palms, but you have been probably assuming that **the person-who-has-the-power-to-hire-you** will be sitting there *enjoying* this whole masochistic process. That is sometimes, but rarely, true.

No, no, you do not have one individual *(you)* sitting there, scared to death, in the hiring-interview.

You have two individuals *(you* and *the employer)* sitting there, scared to death. It's just that the employer has learned to *hide* his or her fears better than you have, because they've had more practice.

But he or she is, after all, a human being just like you are. He or she may *never* have been hired to do *this. This* just got thrown in with all their other duties. And they may *know* they're not very good at it.

It will help give you confidence if you mentally catalog ahead of time *not your fears, but the employer's.* They include:

A. That you won't be able to do the job: that you lack the necessary skills or experience, and the hiring-interview didn't uncover this.

B. That if hired, you won't put in a full working day, regularly.

C. That if hired, you'll be frequently "out sick," or otherwise absent whole days.

D. That if hired, you'll only stay around for a few weeks or at most a few months, and then quit without advance warning.

E. That it will take you too long to master the job, and thus it will be too long before you're profitable to that organization.

F. That you won't get along with the other workers there, or that you will develop a personality conflict with the boss himself (or herself).

G. That you will do only the minimum that you can get away with, rather than the maximum that they hired you for.

H. That you will always have to be told what to do next, rather than displaying initiative -- always in a responding mode, rather than an initiating mode (and mood).

I. That you will have a work-disrupting character flaw, and turn out to be: dishonest, or totally irresponsible, a spreader of dissension at work, lazy, an embezzler, a gossip, a sexual harasser, a drug-user or substance abuser, a drunk, a liar, incompetent, or -- in a word -- bad news.

J. *(If this is a large organization, and your would-be boss is not the top person)*: that you will bring discredit upon them, and upon their department/section/division, etc., for ever hiring you in the first place -- making them lose face, possibly also costing your would-be boss a raise or promotion.

K. That you will cost a lot of money, if they make a mistake by hiring you. Currently, in the U.S. the cost to an employer of a bad hire can run $50,000 or more, including relocation costs, lost pay for the period for work not done or aborted, and severance pay -- if *they* let you go.

No wonder the employer is sweating.

In the old days, an employer might have gotten useful information to guide them in the hiring decision, from *outside* the hiring-interview, by obtaining references from your previous employers. No more. In the past decade, as job-hunters have started filing lawsuits left and right, alleging 'unlawful discharge,' or 'being deprived of an ability to make a living,' more than half of all *Previous Employers* have adopted the policy of refusing to volunteer *any* information about Past Employees, except name, rank, and serial number -- i.e., the person's job-title and dates of employment.

The interviewer is therefore completely on his own -- or her own -- in trying to figure out, *during this interview, or during a series of interviews* -- whether or not to hire you. The hiring interview these days has become *everything*.

FOURTH COMFORTING THOUGHT: YOU DON'T HAVE TO MEMORIZE A LOT OF ANSWERS

To help them figure out whether or not to hire you, they will be asking you some questions. Books on interviewing, of which there are many, often publish lists of these questions -- or at least some *typical* ones that employers ask, such as:

- Tell me about yourself.
- Why are you applying for this job?
- What do you know about this job or company?
- How would you describe yourself?
- What are your major strengths?
- What is your greatest weakness?
- What type of work do you like to do best?
- What are your interests outside of work?
- What accomplishment gave you the greatest satisfaction?
- What was your worst mistake in previous jobs?
- Why did you leave your last job?
- Why were you fired (if you were)?
- How does your education or experience relate to this job?
- Where do you see yourself five years from now?
- What are your goals in life?
- How much did you make at your last job?

Well, the list goes on and on. It sometimes totals eighty-nine questions, or more.

You are then told that you should prepare for a hiring-interview by writing out, practicing, and memorizing some clever answers to *all* these questions -- answers which some books furnish for you. Well, not the best advice.

Dear friend, your preparation for the hiring-interview does not need to be that complicated.

Beneath the dozens and dozens of possible questions like those above that employers could ask you, there are really only *five basic questions,* that you need to remember.

Five. Just five. And they are:

The person-who-has-the-power-to-hire-you wants to know:

1. "Why are you here?" *They mean by this, "Why are you knocking on my door, rather than someone else's door?"*

Then, the person-who-has-the-power-to-hire-you wants to know:

2. "What can you do for us?" *They mean by this, "If I were to hire you would you be part of the problems I already have, or would you be a part of the solution to those problems? What are your skills, and how much do you know about some subject or field that is of interest to us?"*

Then, the person-who-has-the-power-to-hire-you wants to know:

3. "What kind of person are you?" *They mean by this, "Do you have the kind of personality that makes it easy for people to work with you, and do you share the values which we have at this place?"*

Then, the person-who-has-the-power-to-hire-you wants to know:

4. "What distinguishes you from nineteen other people who can do the same tasks that you can?" *They mean by this, "Do you have better work habits than the nineteen others, do you show up earlier, stay later, work more thoroughly, work faster, maintain higher standards, go the extra mile, or . . . what?"*

Lastly, the person-who-has-the-power-to-hire-you wants to know:

5. "Can I afford you?" *They mean by this, "If we decide we want you here, how much will it take to get you, and are we willing and able to pay that amount -- governed, as we are, by our budget, and by our inability to pay you as much as the person who would be above you, on the organizational chart?"*

These are the five *main* questions that *bug* employers most. *This is the case, even if the interview begins and ends with these five questions never once being uttered aloud.* They're still floating in the room there, beneath the surface of the conversation, beneath the eighty-nine questions they may ask.

The good news is that since there are really only five basic questions on the employer's mind, and not eighty-nine, there are really only five answers you need to know.

But, you had *better* know those five answers. If you did your homework in Chapters 5 and 6 plus the Workbook on page 7, you will. If you didn't, you won't. Period. End of story.

You, of course, have the right -- nay, the duty -- to be asking yourself the same five questions, in only a slightly different form:

1. What does this job involve?

2. Do my skills truly match this job?

3. Are these the kind of people I would like to work with, or

not? *Do not ignore your intuition if it tells you that you would not be comfortable working with these people!!*

4. If we like each other, and both want to work together, can I persuade them there is something unique about me, that makes me different from nineteen other people who can do the same tasks?

5. Can I persuade them to hire me at the salary I need or want?

You don't, of course, ask these questions in the interview. Rather, you might begin your part of the hiring-interview by reporting to them just exactly how you've been conducting your job-hunt, and what impressed you so much about *their* organization during your research, that you decided to come in and talk to them about a job. Then you can devote your attention, during the remainder of the interview, to exploring the five questions above, in your own way.[5]

If you're not there about a job that already exists, but rather, you want them to *create* a job for you, then your five questions get changed into five *statements*, that you make to this person-who-has-the-power-to-hire-you:

1. What you **like** about this organization.

2. What sorts of **needs** you find intriguing in this field and in this organization (don't ever use the word "*problems*," as most employers prefer synonyms, such as '*needs*'-- unless you first hear the word '*problems*' coming out of their mouth).

3. What **skills** seem to you to be needed in order to meet such needs.

4. **Evidence** from your past experience that demonstrates you have the very skills in question, and that you perform them in the manner or style you claim.

5. What is **unique** about the way *you* perform those skills. As I have mentioned before, this is something you *must* devote

---

5. Additional questions you may want to ask, to elaborate upon these five:
   What significant changes has this company gone through in the last five years?
   What values are sacred to this company?
   What characterizes the most successful employees this company has?
   What future changes do you see in the work here?
   Who do you see as your allies, colleagues, or competitors in this business?

some thought to, ahead of time. For example, if you analyze problems, how do you do that? *Painstakingly? Intuitively, in a flash? By consulting with greater authorities in the field?* You see the point. You are trying to put your finger on the 'style' or 'manner' in which you do your work, that is distinctive and hopefully appealing, to this employer.

I have said this before, but I will say it again: every prospective employer wants to know *what makes you different* from nineteen other people who can do the same kind of work as you do. You *have* to know what that is. And then not only talk about it, but actually demonstrate it, by the way you conduct your part of the hiring-interview. *E.g., "I am very thorough in the way I would do the job for you"* = be thorough in the way you have researched the place before you go in for the hiring-interview.

FIFTH COMFORTING THOUGHT: THE EMPLOYER DOESN'T REALLY CARE ABOUT YOUR PAST

In most cases, as I have been emphasizing, the person-who-has-the-power-to-hire-you is *scared.* If you think that is too strong a word, let's settle for *anxious,* or *afraid,* or *worried.* And this worry lies beneath all the questions they may ask.

Their fear, by definition, is about the future. No employer cares about your past. In fact, in the U.S., employers must only ask you questions related to the requirements and expectations of the job. They cannot ask about such things in your past (or present) as your creed, religion, race, age, sexual orientation, or marital status.

Rules aside, you must realize that the only thing any employer should possibly care about is your future . . . with *them.* But the future is difficult to uncover, so they usually try to gauge your future behavior by asking about your past behavior.

Do not be fooled by this absorption with your past. Your whole focus during the time the employer is questioning you should be to sense what fear about the *future* lies beneath each question that the employer asks you concerning your past -- and then answer that fear.

Here are some *examples:*

Employer's Question	The Fear Behind The Question	The Point You Try To Get Across	Phrases You Might Use To Get This Across
"Tell me about yourself"	The employer is afraid he/she isn't going to conduct a very good interview, by failing to ask the right questions. Or is afraid there is some-thing wrong with you, and is hoping you will blurt it out.	You are a good employee, as you have proved in the past at your other jobs. (Give the brief-est history of who you are, where born, raised, interests, hobbies, and kind of work you have en-joyed the most to date.) *Keep it to two minutes, max.*	In describing your past work history, use any *honest* phrases you can about your work history, that are self-complimentary: "Hard worker." "Came in early, left late." "Always did more than was ex-pected of me." Etc.
"What kind of work are you looking for?"	The employer is afraid that you are look-ing for a dif-ferent job than that which the employer is trying to fill. E.g., he/she wants a secre-tary, but you want to be an office manager, etc.	You are looking for precisely the kind of work the employer is offering (but don't say that, if it isn't true). Repeat back to the employer, in your own words, what he/she has said about the job, and emphasize the skills you have to do *that*.	If the employer hasn't described the job at all, say, 'I'd be happy to answer that, but first I need to understand exactly what kind of work this job involves." *Then* answer, as at left.
"Have you ever done this kind of work before?"	The employer is afraid you don't possess the necessary skills and ex-perience to do this job.	You have skills that are trans-ferable, from whatever you used to do; and you did it well.	"I pick up stuff very quickly." "I have quickly mastered any job I have ever done."

Employer's Question	The Fear Behind The Question	The Point You Try To Get Across	Phrases You Might Use To Get This Across
"When did you leave your last job?" -- *or* "How did you get along with your former boss and co-workers?"	The employer is afraid you don't get along well with people, especially bosses, and is just waiting for you to 'bad-mouth' your previous boss- or co-workers, as proof of that.	Say whatever positive things you possibly can about your former boss and co-workers (*without telling lies*). Emphasize you usually get along very well with people -- and then let your gracious attitude toward your previous boss(es) and co-workers prove it, right before this employer's very eyes (and ears).	If you left voluntarily: "*My boss and I* both felt I would be happier and more effective in a job where [here describe your strong points, such as] I would have more room to use my initiative and creativity." If you were fired: "Usually, I get along well with everyone, but in this particular case the boss and I just didn't get along with each other. Difficult to say why." *You don't need to say any more than that.* If you were laid off and your job wasn't filled after you left: "My *job* was terminated."
"How is your health?" -- *or* "How much were you absent from work during your last job?"	The employer is afraid you will be absent from work a lot, if they hire you.	You will not be absent. If you have a health problem, you want to emphasize that it is one which will not keep you from being at work, daily. Your productivity, compared to other workers', is excellent.	If you were *not* absent a lot at your last job: "I believe it's an employee's job to show up every work day. Period." If you *were* absent a lot, say why, and stress that it was due to a difficulty that is now *past*.

Employer's Question	The Fear Behind The Question	The Point You Try To Get Across	Phrases You Might Use To Get This Across
"Can you explain why you've been out of work so long?" -- or "Can you tell me why there are these gaps in your work history?" *(Usually said after studying your resume.)*	The employer is afraid that you are the kind of person who quits a job the minute he/she doesn't like something at it; in other words, that you have no 'stick-to-it-iveness.'	You love to work, and you regard times when things aren't going well as challenges, which you enjoy learning how to conquer.	"During the gaps in my work record, I was studying/doing volunteer work/doing some hard thinking about my mission in life/finding redirection." (Choose one.)
"Wouldn't this job represent a step down for you?" -- or "I think this job would be way beneath your talents and experience." -- or "Don't you think you would be underemployed if you took this job?"	The employer is afraid you could command a bigger salary, somewhere else, and will therefore leave him/her as soon as something better turns up.	You will stick with this job as long as you and the employer agree this is where you should be.	"This job isn't a step down for me. It's a step up -- from welfare." "We have mutual fears: every employer is afraid a good employee will leave too soon, and every employee is afraid the employer might fire him/her, for no good reason." "I like to work, and I give my best to every job I've ever had."
And, lastly: "Tell me, what is your greatest weakness?"	The employer is afraid you have some character flaw, and hopes you will now rashly blurt it out, or confess it.	You have limitations just like anyone else but you work constantly to improve yourself and be a more and more effective worker.	Mention a weakness and then stress its positive aspect, e.g., "I don't like to be oversupervised, because I have a great deal of initiative, and I like to anticipate problems before they even arise."

As the interview proceeds, you want to quietly notice (*but not comment on*) the *time-sequence* of the questions the employer is asking. When the interview is turning out favorably for you, the time-sequence of the employer's questions will often move -- *however slowly* -- through the following stages.

1. Distant past: *e.g., "Where did you attend high school?"*

2. Immediate past: *e.g., "Tell me about your most recent job."*

3. Present: *e.g., "What kind of a job are you looking for?"*

4. Immediate future: *e.g., "Would you be able to come back for another interview next week?"*

5. [*Optional:* Distant future: *e.g., "Where would you like to be five years from now?"*]

The more the interviewer's questions move from the past to the future, the more favorably the interview is going for you. On the other hand, if the interviewer's questions stay firmly in the past, the outlook is not so good. *Ah well, y' can't win them all!*

If the time-frame of the interviewer's questions moves firmly into the future, *then* is the time for you to get more specific about the job. Experts suggest you ask these kinds of questions:

What is the job, specifically, that I am being considered for?

If I were hired, what duties would I be performing?

What responsibilities would I have?

What would you be hiring me to accomplish?

Would I be working with a team, or group? To whom would I report?

Whose responsibility is it to see that I get the training I need, here, to get up to speed?

How would I be evaluated, how often, and by whom?

What were the strengths and weaknesses of previous people in this position?

Why did *you* yourself decide to work here?

What do you wish you had known about this company before you started here? What particular characteristics do you think have made you successful in your job here?

May I meet the person I would be working for (if it isn't you)?

Remember, throughout this *weighing of each other*, we're not talking scientific measurement here. As Nathan Azrin has said for many years, *The hiring process is more like choosing a mate, than*

it is like deciding whether or not to buy a new house. This of course is not to be taken literally. To say that hiring is like choosing a mate does not mean that if you get hired, you will literally be marrying the organization or someone in the organization. No, no, no.

'Choosing a mate' here is a metaphor. To elaborate upon the metaphor a little bit, it means that *the mechanisms* by which human nature decides to hire someone, are *similar to* the mechanisms by which human nature decides whether or not to marry someone. Those mechanisms, of course, are impulsive, intuitional, non-rational, and often made on the spur of the moment -- often revolving around some small idiotic *oops,* that only their sister Ann would understand.

SIXTH COMFORTING THOUGHT: INTERVIEWS ARE OFTEN LOST IN THE FIRST TWO MINUTES

To continue our discussion of the metaphor of *choosing a mate and hiring,* think about this: you can have all the skills in the world, have researched this organization to death, have practiced *interviewing* until you are a master at giving 'right answers,' be absolutely the perfect person for this job, and yet lose the hiring-interview because . . . *your breath smells terrible.* Or some other small personal reason. It's akin to your being ready to fight dragons, and then being killed by a mosquito.

"I'll tell you why I want this job. I thrive on challenges. I like being stretched to my full capacity. I like solving problems. Also, my car is about to be repossessed."

It's the reason why interviews are most often lost, when they are lost, *during the first two minutes.*

Let me hold in abeyance, for a moment or two, my strange claim, above, that this is *a comforting thought.* And let us first look at *what* interview-mosquitoes (*as it were*) can fly in, during the first 30 seconds to two minutes of your interview with *the person-who-has-the-power-to-hire-you,* so that they start muttering to themselves, *"I sure hope we have some other candidates besides this person"*:

1. Your appearance and personal habits: interview after interview has revealed that if you are a male, *you are much more likely to get the job if --*

• you have obviously freshly bathed, have your face freshly shaved or your hair and beard freshly trimmed, have clean fingernails; and are using a deodorant;

• you have on freshly laundered clothes, and a suit rather than a sports outfit, pants with a sharp crease, and shoes freshly polished;

• you do not have bad breath, do not dispense gallons of garlic, onion, stale tobacco, or the odor of strong drink, into the enclosed office air; but have brushed and flossed your teeth, plus used a mouthwash if necessary;

• you are not wafting tons of after-shave cologne fifteen feet ahead of you, as you enter the room.

Remember, since the hiring process is more like choosing a mate, than deciding whether or not to buy a new house, the employer is simply trying to determine if they like you. If you 'bomb' in one of these areas just listed, the person-who-has-the-power-to-hire-you may decide they really don't like you, in which case you're not going to get hired there, no matter how qualified you otherwise may be.

If you are a female, interview after interview has revealed that *you are much more likely to get the job if --*

• you have obviously freshly bathed, have not got tons of makeup on your face; have had your hair newly 'permed' or 'coiffed'; have clean or nicely manicured fingernails, that don't stick out ten inches from your fingers; and are using a deodorant;

• you wear a bra, have on freshly cleaned clothes, a suit or sophisticated-looking dress, shoes not sandals, and ones which don't call *a lot* of attention to themselves;

• you do not have bad breath, do not dispense gallons of garlic, onion, stale tobacco, or the odor of strong drink, into the enclosed office air; but have brushed and flossed your teeth, plus used a mouthwash if necessary;

• you are not wafting tons of perfume fifteen feet ahead of you, as you enter the room.

Remember, since the hiring process is more like choosing a mate, than deciding whether or not to buy a new house, the employer is simply trying to determine if they like you. If you 'bomb' in one of these areas just listed, the person-who-has-the-power-to-hire-you may decide they really don't like you, in which case you're not going to get hired there, no matter how qualified you otherwise may be.

2. Nervous mannerisms: *it is a turn-off for employers if --*

• you give a limp handshake, *or*

• you slouch in your chair, or endlessly fidget in your seat, during the interview, *or*

• you continually avoid eye contact with the employer, *or*

• you crack your knuckles, *or* are constantly playing with your hands, or your hair.

Remember, since the hiring process is more like choosing a mate, than deciding whether or not to buy a new house, the employer is simply trying to determine if they like you. If you 'bomb' in one of these areas just listed, the person-who-has-the-power-to-hire-you may decide they really don't like you, in which case you're not going to get hired there, no matter how qualified you otherwise may be.

3. Lack of self-confidence: *it is a turn-off for employers if--*

• you are continuously being extremely self-critical,

• you are downplaying your achievements or abilities,

• you are speaking so softly you cannot be heard, or so loudly you can be heard two rooms away,

• you are giving one-word answers to all the employer's questions,

• you are constantly interrupting the employer,

• or you are giving answers in an extremely hesitant fashion.

Remember, since the hiring process is more like choosing a mate, than deciding whether or not to buy a new house, the employer is simply trying to determine if they like you. If you 'bomb' in one of these areas just listed, the person-who-has-the-power-to-hire-you may decide they really don't like you, in which case you're not going to get hired there, no matter how qualified you otherwise may be.

4. Your considerateness toward other people: *it is a turn-off for employers if--*

• you show a lack of courtesy to the receptionist, secretary, and (at lunch) to the waiter or waitress,

• you display extreme criticalness toward your previous employers and places of work,

• you drink strong stuff (ordering a drink if and when the employer takes you to lunch is always a bad idea, as it raises the question in the employer's mind, *Do they normally stop with one, or do they normally keep on going?* Don't . . . do . . . it!)

• you forget to thank the interviewer as you're leaving, or forget to send a thank-you note afterward. Says one human resources manager: "A prompt, brief, faxed business letter thanking me for my time along with a (brief!) synopsis of his/

her unique qualities communicates to me that this person is an assertive, motivated, customer service-oriented salesperson who utilizes technology and knows the rules of the 'game.' These are qualities I am looking for. At the moment I receive approximately one letter for every fifteen candidates interviewed."

Remember, since the hiring process is more like choosing a mate, than deciding whether or not to buy a new house, the employer is simply trying to determine if they like you. If you 'bomb' in one of these areas just listed, the person-who-has-the-power-to-hire-you may decide they really don't like you, in which case you're not going to get hired there, no matter how qualified you otherwise may be.

• Incidentally, *many* an employer watches to see if you smoke, either in the office or at lunch. *(In a race between two equally qualified people, the nonsmoker will win out over the smoker 94% of the time, according to a study done by a professor of business at Seattle University.) Some experts give the following advice to smokers who are therefore determined to hide the fact that they smoke from the interviewer: "If you are a smoker, do not think it will be easy to hide it. It will take a lot of work, on your part. The more that smoke has been hovering around you and your clothes, the more your clothes, hair, and breath will reek of smoke when you go in for the interview. You are so inured to it, that you will not be able to detect this; but the employer will know it,* instantly, *as you move forward to greet them. Breath mints and perfume/cologne will NOT cover it up; it will take much*

more formidable measures than that. Like what? Like this: don't smoke for at least four hours prior to the interview, bathe completely, including your hair, immediately before leaving for the interview, keep a set of smoke-free interview clothes, underwear, and shoes (at home) in a tight plastic bag in a room far-removed from any place you smoke in the house, and wear those smoke-free clothes to the interview." That's the advice of the You-Can-Hide-It school of thinking. Personally, I think all such deceptions practiced upon the employer are, in the end, self-defeating. So what if you do pull it off? It will come out that you smoke, after you are hired, and the employer who hates smoking can always manage to get you out of there after you are hired, on one pretext or another, without ever mentioning the word 'smoke.' So, don't try to hide it. Nonetheless, wait to reveal it. Never smoke during the time you are with the person-who-has-the-power-to-hire-you, unless they are smoking like a chimney themselves; -- and so as to prevent yourself from having to run out and take 'a smoke break,' I'd suggest you take chewing gum (or nicotine patches) with you to the interview, as you may be stuck there a long time). Once a job-offer has been made, then I think it is important for you to tell the employer you smoke, and to offer an easy way out: "If this is a truly offensive habit to you, and one you don't want in any of your employees, I'd rather bow out gracefully now, than have it become an issue between us down the road." Such consideration, thoughtfulness, and graciousness on your part may go a long way to soften the employer's resistance to the fact that you are a smoker. Many places, in fact, allow their employees to go outside for a 'smoke break' at stated intervals.

   5. Your values: *it is a complete turn-off for most employers, if they see in you* --
   • any signs of dishonesty or lying, on your resume or in the interview;
   • any signs of irresponsibility or tendency to goof off;
   • any sign of arrogance or excessive aggressiveness; any sign of tardiness or failure to keep appointments and commitments on time, including the hiring-interview;
   • any sign of not following instructions or obeying rules;
   • any sign of constant complaining or blaming things on others;

- any sign of laziness or lack of motivation;
- any sign of a lack of enthusiasm for this organization and what it is trying to do;
- any sign of instability, inappropriate response, and the like.
- the other ways in which you evidence your *values*, such as: what things impress you or don't impress you in the office; what you are willing to sacrifice in order to get this job *and* what you are *not* willing to sacrifice in order to get this job; your enthusiasm for work;
- the carefulness with which you did or didn't research this company before you came in;

and blah, blah, blah.

Remember, since the hiring process is more like choosing a mate, than deciding whether or not to buy a new house, the employer is simply trying to determine if they like you. If you 'bomb' in one of these areas just listed, the person-who-has-the-power-to-hire-you may decide they really don't like you, in which case you're not going to get hired there, no matter how qualified you otherwise may be.

Anyway, these are the *mosquitoes* that can kill you, when you're out to fight dragons, in the hiring-interview.

Now please, dear friend, do not write me, telling me how picayune some of this is. Believe me, I already *know* that. I'm not reporting the world as it *should* be. I'm only reporting what study after study has revealed about the world as it *is*.

You may take this all to heart, or just ignore it. However, if you decide to ignore these points, and then -- despite interview after interview -- you never get hired, you might want to rethink your position on all of this. It may be the mosquitoes, not the dragons, that are killing you.

And you can *fix* these mosquitoes. That's why I said, back at the beginning of *this* section: that the fact the interview can thus be lost in the first two minutes over such picayune things as *these*, is a *comforting* thought. It's comforting, because *all* of these picayune things *are in your control*. Yes, you control *every one* of these factors.

Read them all over again. There isn't a one of them that you don't have the power to determine, or the power to change. You can decide to bathe before going to the interview, you can decide to shine your shoes, you can decide not to smoke, etc., etc. All the little things which could torpedo your interview are within your control, and *you can fix* them, if they are keeping you from getting hired.

I'd say that was a comforting thought, wouldn't you?

How
To End The Inteview

Before you let the interview end, there are six questions you should *always* ask:

#1. *"Given my skills and experience, is there work here that you would consider me for?"* This is if you haven't come after a specific job, from the beginning.

#2. *"Can you offer me this job?"* I know this seems stupid, but it is astonishing how many job-hunters have secured a job simply by being bold enough to ask for it, at the end of the interview, either with the words *May I have this job,* or something similar to it, in language they feel comfortable with. I don't know *why* this is so. I only know *that* it is so. Maybe it has something to do with employers not liking to say "No," to someone who directly asks them for something. Anyway, if after hearing all about this job at this place, you decide you'd really like to have it, *ask for it.* The worst thing the employer can say is "No," or "We need some time to think about all the interviews we're conducting."

#3. *"Do you want me to come back for another interview, perhaps with some of your colleagues here?"* If you are a serious candidate, in this employer's mind, for this job, there usually *is* a second round of interviews. And, often, a third, and fourth. You, of course, want to be in that second round. Indeed, many experts say the *only* purpose you should have in the first interview, at a particular place, is to be invited back for a second interview. If you've secured *that*, say they, it has been a successful first interview.

#4. *"When may I expect to hear from you?"* You *never* want to leave control of the ensuing steps in this process in the hands of the employer. You want it in your own hands. If the employer says, *"We need time to think about this,"* or *"We will be calling you for a second interview,"* you don't want to leave this as an undated good intention on the employer's part. You want to nail it down.

#5. *"What would be the latest I can expect to hear from you?"* The employer has probably given you their *best* guess, in answer to your previous question. Now you want to know *what is the worst-case* scenario? One employer, when I asked him the *worst-case* scenario replied, *"Never!"* I thought he had a great sense of humor. Turned out he was dead serious.

#6. *"May I contact you after that date, if for any reason you haven't gotten back to me by that time?"* Some employers resent this question. You'll know that is the case if they snap at you, *"Don't you trust me?"* But most employers appreciate your offering them what is in essence a safety-net. They know they can get busy, become overwhelmed with other things, forget their promise to you. It's reassuring, in such a case, for you to offer to rescue them.

[Optional: #7. *"Can you think of anyone else who might be interested in hiring me?"* This question is invoked *only* if they replied *"No,"* to your first question, above.]

Jot down any answers they give you to the questions above, then stand up, thank them sincerely for their time, give a firm handshake, and leave. Write a thank-you note *that night*, to them, and mail it without fail the next morning.

In the following days, rigorously keep to this covenant, and don't contact them except with that mandatory thank-you note, until after the *latest* deadline you two agreed upon, in answer to question #4, above. If you do have to contact them after that date, and if they tell you things are still up in the air, you ask questions #3, #4, and #5, all over again. And so on, and so forth.

Incidentally, it is entirely appropriate for you to insert a thank-you note into the running stream, after *each* interview or telephone contact. That will help them remember you.

How
(And When) To Negotiate Your Salary

Assuming things went favorably in the first interview, and assuming they weren't ready at that time to point-blank offer you the job, you *will* be invited back for another interview, *or interviews* at that place -- either with the person you saw before, and/or with a committee. Eventually, after the second, third, or fourth interview, if *you* like them and *they* increasingly like you, a job offer *will* be made.

Then, and only then, it is time to deal with the question that is inevitably on any employer's mind -- as we saw on page 192 -- *how much is this person going to cost me?* And the question that is on *your* mind: *how much does this job pay?*

It's time for salary negotiation. While whole books can be (and have been) written on this subject, there are basically just five keys for you to keep in mind:

THE EMPLOYER WILL RARELY TELL YOU
THE MOST THEY ARE WILLING TO PAY

Salary negotiation would never happen if *every* employer in *every* hiring-interview were to mention, right from the start, the top figure they are willing to pay for that position. *Some* employers do. And that's the end of any salary negotiation. But, of course, most of them don't. Hoping they'll be able to get you for less, they start *lower* than they're ultimately willing to go. This creates *a range.* And that range is what salary negotiation is all about.

For example, if the employer wants to hire somebody for no more than $12 an hour, they may start *the bidding* at $8 an hour. In which case, their *range* runs from $8 to $12 an hour. Or if they want to pay no more than $20 an hour, they may start the bidding at $16 an hour. In which case their range runs from $16 to $20 an hour.

So, why do you have to negotiate? Because, if a range *is* thus involved, you have every right to try to negotiate the highest salary possible *within that range.*

The employer's goal, is to save money, if possible. Your goal is to bring home to your family, your partner, or your own household, the best salary that you can, for the work you will be doing. Nothing's wrong with the goals of either of you. But it does mean that, where the employer starts lower, salary negotiation is proper, and expected.

NEVER DISCUSS SALARY UNTIL THE END
OF THE INTERVIEWING PROCESS, WHEN THEY HAVE
DEFINITELY SAID THEY WANT YOU

If the employer raises the salary question earlier, but seems like a kindly man or woman, your best reply might be: "Until you've decided you definitely want me, and I've decided I definitely could help you with your tasks here, I feel any discussion of salary is premature." That will work, in most cases.

But suppose you are face-to-face with an employer, and they *demand* to know what salary you are looking for, within the first two minutes that you're in the room. You try the excellent response you rehearsed, for this very eventuality: "I'll gladly come to that, but could you first help me to understand what this job involves?"

Good response, *in most cases*. But this time it doesn't work. The employer with rising voice says, "Come, come, don't play games with me. I want to know what salary you're looking for." You have a response prepared for *this* eventuality, too. You answer in terms of a *range*, but this employer insists on a single figure. "How much per hour?" they bark.

In today's market, many interviews begin here, and this is increasingly where many interviews end. The employer has no range in mind. The beginning figure is the ending figure. No negotiation is possible.[6]

This happens, when it happens, because many employers are making salary their major criterion for deciding who to hire, and who not to hire, out of -- say -- nineteen possible candidates.

If you run into this situation, and you want that job badly enough, you have no choice but to capitulate. Ask what they are offering, and make your decision. (Of course you may always say, *"I need a little time, to think about this."*)

However, this is the *worst-case scenario*. Things don't always go this way. Not by a long shot. In lots and lots of interviews, these days, salary is still negotiable -- *if you save the discussion to the very end of the interviewing process.*

---

6. One job-hunter said his interviews *always* began with the salary question, and no matter what he answered, that ended the interview. Turned out, this job-hunter was doing all the interviewing *over the phone*. That was the problem. Once he went *face-to-face*, salary was no longer the first thing discussed in the interview.

When To Negotiate Salary[7]

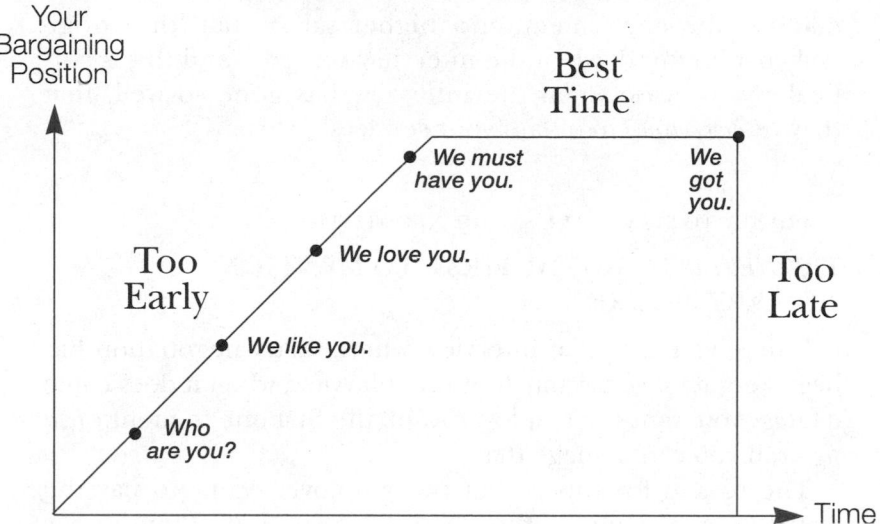

Your Bargaining Position

Best Time

We must have you.

We got you.

Too Early

We love you.

Too Late

We like you.

Who are you?

Time

Don't Discuss Salary

Until all of the following conditions have been fulfilled --

- Not until they've gotten to know you, at your best, so they can see how you stand out above the other applicants.
- Not until you've gotten to know them, as completely as you can, so you can tell when they're being firm, or when they're flexible.
- Not until you've found out exactly what the job entails.
- Not until they've had a chance to find out how well you match the job-requirements.
- Not until you're in the final interview at that place, for that job.
- Not until you've decided, "I'd really like to work here."
- Not until they've said, "We want you."
- Not until they've said, "We've got to have you."

-- should you get into salary discussion with this employer.

---

7. Reprinted, by permission of the publisher, from *Ready, Aim, You're Hired*, by Paul Hellman, © 1986 Paul Hellman. Published by AMACOM, a division of American Management Association, New York. All rights reserved.

Why is it to your advantage to delay salary discussion? Because, if you really *shine* during the hiring-interview, they may -- at the end -- mention a higher salary than they originally had in mind, when the interview started -- and this is particularly the case when the interview has gone so well, that they're *determined* to obtain your services.

THIRD KEY TO SUCCESSFUL SALARY NEGOTIATION:

TRY *NEVER* TO BE THE FIRST TO MENTION A SALARY FIGURE

Where you are in an interview where salary negotiation has been kept *off stage* for much of the interview, when it does come *on stage* you want the employer to be the first one to mention *a figure,* if you can manage that.

The reason for this is that the employer wants to pay the least they can, while on the other hand you want them to pay the most they can, *within their range.* So, it's going to be a kind of verbal arm-wrestling. And, never mind the reason why, what has been observed over the years is that in this contest *whoever mentions a salary figure first, generally loses salary negotiation, at the last.*

Inexperienced employer/interviewers don't know this. Experienced ones do; that's why they will *always* toss the ball to you, with some innocent-sounding question, such as: "What kind of salary are you looking for?" *Well, how kind of them to ask me what I want* -- you may be thinking. No, no, no. Kindness has nothing to do with it. They are hoping *you* will be the first to mention a figure, because they know this obscure rule well, that *whoever mentions a salary figure first, generally loses salary negotiation, at the last.*

So of course, you will *always* want to respond, if you can: "Well, you created this position, so you must have some figure in mind, and I'd be interested in knowing what that is."

FOURTH KEY TO SUCCESSFUL SALARY NEGOTIATION:

BEFORE YOU GO TO THE INTERVIEW, DO HOMEWORK ON HOW MUCH YOU NEED.

When you are in an interview process where salary discussion is indeed saved *(as it should be)* to the end, salary negotiation *within their range* is wide open -- *except* for this one horrible scenario: *What if* their *highest figure is so far below* your *lowest figure, that you will starve, if you accept it?* You need $14 an hour, to barely survive, and the highest they are willing to pay is $8 an hour.

You see the problem. You've *got* to know, beforehand, just how much it is you need to make, at a minimum.

You can determine this in one of two ways: a) take a wild guess -- and risk finding out after you take the job that it's simply impossible for you to live on that salary *(the favorite strategy in this country, and most others)*; or, b) make out a detailed outline of your estimated expenses *now*, listing what you need *monthly* in the following categories:[8]

---

8. If this kind of financial figuring is not your cup of tea, find a buddy, friend, relative, family member, or *anyone*, who can help you do this. If you don't know anyone who could do this, go to your local church, synagogue, religious center, social club, gym, or wherever you hang out, and ask the leader or manager there, to help you find someone. If there's a bulletin board, put up a notice on the bulletin board.

Housing

    Rent or mortgage payments . . . . $ _____

    Electricity/gas . . . . $ _____

    Water . . . . $ _____

    Telephone . . . . $ _____

    Garbage removal . . . . $ _____

    Cleaning, maintenance, repairs[9] . . . . $ _____

Food

    What you spend at the supermarket

        and/or meat market, etc. . . . . $ _____

    Eating out . . . . $ _____

Clothing

    Purchase of new or used clothing . . . . $ _____

    Cleaning, dry cleaning, laundry . . . . $ _____

Automobile/transportation[10]

    Car payments . . . . $ _____

    Gas . . . . $ _____

    Repairs . . . . $ _____

    Public transportation *(bus, train, plane)* . . . . . . $ _____

Insurance

    Car . . . . $ _____

    Medical or health-care . . . . $ _____

    House and personal possessions . . . . $ _____

    Life . . . . $ _____

Medical expenses

    Doctors' visits . . . . $ _____

    Prescriptions . . . . $ _____

    Fitness costs . . . . $ _____

---

9. If you have extra household expenses, such as a security system for example, be sure and include the quarterly (or whatever) expenses here, divided by three.

10. Your checkbook stubs will tell you a lot of this stuff. But you may be vague about your cash or credit card expenditures. For example, you may not know how much you spend at the supermarket, or how much you spend on gas, etc. But there is a simple way to find out. Just carry a little notepad and pen around with you for two weeks or more, and jot down *everything* you pay cash *(or use credit cards)* for -- *on the spot, right after you pay it.* At the end of those two weeks, you'll be able to take that notepad and make a realistic guess of what should be put down in these categories that now puzzle you. *(Multiply the two-weeks figure by two, and you'll have the monthly figure.)*

Support for Other Family Members
    Child-care costs *(if you have children)*. . . . . $ _____
    Child-support *(if you're paying that)* . . . . $ _____
    Support for your parents *(if you're helping out)*. $ _____
Charity giving/tithe *(to help others)* . . . . $ _____
School/learning
    Children's costs *(if you have children in school)*. . $ _____
    Your learning costs *(adult education,*
        job-hunting classes, etc.) . . . . $ _____
Pet care *(if you have pets)* . . . . $ _____
Bills and debts *(usual monthly payments)*
    Credit cards. . . . . $ _____
    Local stores . . . . $ _____
    Other obligations you pay off monthly . . . . . . $ _____
Taxes
    Federal[11] *(next April's due, divided by*
        months remaining until then). . . . . $ _____
    State *(likewise)* . . . . $ _____
    Local/property *(next amount due, divided by*
        months remaining until then). . . . . $ _____
    Tax-help *(if you ever use an accountant,*
        pay a friend to help you with taxes, etc.). . . . . . . $ _____
Savings. . . . . $ _____
Retirement (Keogh, IRA, SEP, etc.) . . . . $ _____
Amusement/discretionary spending
    Movies, video rentals, etc.. . . . . $ _____
    Other kinds of entertainment . . . . $ _____
    Reading, newspapers, magazines, books . . . . . $ _____
    Gifts *(birthday, Christmas, etc.)* . . . . $ _____

Total Amount You Need Each Month . . . . $ _____

---

11. Incidentally, looking ahead to next April 15th, be sure and check with your local IRS office or a reputable accountant to find out if you can deduct the expenses of your job-hunt on your Federal (and State) income tax returns. At this writing, some job-hunters can, if -- big IF -- this is not your first job that you're looking for, if you haven't been unemployed too long, and if you aren't making a career-change. Do go find out what the latest "if"s are. If IRS tells you you are eligible, keep careful receipts of everything related to your job-hunt, as you go along: telephone calls, stationery, printing, postage, travel, etc.

Multiply the total amount you need each month by 12, to get the yearly figure. Divide the yearly figure by 2000, and you will be reasonably near the *minimum* hourly wage that you need. Thus, if you need $3333. per month, multiplied by 12 that's $40,000 a year, and then divided by 2,000, that's $20 an hour.

Parenthetically, you may want to prepare two different versions of the above budget: one with the expenses you'd ideally *like* to make, and the other a minimum budget, which will give you what you are looking for, here: the floor, below which you simply cannot afford to go.

BEFORE YOU GO IN, DO RESEARCH ON SALARIES FOR YOUR FIELD AND FOR THAT ORGANIZATION

As I said earlier, salary negotiation is possible *anytime* the employer does not open their discussion of salary by naming the top figure they have in mind, but starts instead with a lower figure.

Okay, so here is our $64,000 question: how do you tell whether the figure the employer first offers you is only their *starting bid,* or is their *final final offer?* The answer is: by doing some research on the field *and* that organization, first.

Oh, come on! I can hear you say. *Isn't this all more trouble than it's worth?* Well, yes, if we were in the chapters on the Impatient Job-Hunter. But this chapter, you recall, is for The Determined Career-Changer or Job-Hunter.

And if you're determined, this is one step you don't want to overlook. Trust me, salary research pays off *handsomely.*

Let's say it takes you from one to three days to run down this sort of information on the three or four organizations that interest you the most. And let us say that because you've done this research, when you finally go in for the hiring-interview you are able to ask for and obtain a salary that is $4,000 a year higher in range, than you would otherwise have gotten. In just the next three years, you will be earning $12,000 extra, because of your salary research. *Not bad pay, for one to three days' work!* And it can be even more. I know *many* job-hunters and career-changers to whom this has happened. Thus you can see that there is a financial penalty exacted from those who are too lazy, or in too much of a hurry, to go gather this information. In plainer language: you don't do this research, it'll cost ya!

Well then, how do you do this research? There's a simple rule: **abandon books, and go talk to people**. Preferably to people who are in the same job *at another company or organization*. Or, go talk to people at the nearby university or college who *train* such people: whatever the department is, where people get trained for this kind of job. These teachers will usually know what their graduates are getting.

Use books, libraries, and the Internet only as a *second*, or *last*, resort. I have listed on page *162* the kind of places on the Internet where you can find salary research. The Internet is particularly helpful in this regard. But talking to people is still your best bet.

Now, exactly how do you go about talking to people, in order to get this information? Let's look at some examples:

> *First Example:* Working at your first entry-level job, say at a fast-food place.

You may not need to do any salary research. They pay what they pay. You can walk in, ask for a job application, and interview with the manager. He or she will usually tell you the pay, outright. It's usually *inflexible*. But at least you'll find it easy to discover what the pay is. (Incidentally, filling out an application, or having an interview there, doesn't commit you to take the job -- but you probably already know that. You can always decline an offer from *any place*. That's what makes this approach harmless.)

> *Second Example:* Working at a place where you can't dis-
> cover what the pay is, say *at a construction company.*

If that construction company where you would *hope* to get a job is difficult to research, go visit a *different* construction company in the same town -- one that isn't of much interest to you -- and ask what they make *there*. Or, if you don't know who to talk to there, fill out one of their applications, and talk to the hiring person about what kinds of jobs they have (or might have in the future), at which time prospective wages is a legitimate subject of discussion. Then, having done this research on a place you don't care about, go back to the place that *really* interests you, and apply. You still don't know *exactly* what they pay, but you do know what their competitor pays -- which will usually be *close*.

> *Third Example:* Working in a one-person office, say *as a secretary.*

Here you can often find useful salary information by perusing the *Help Wanted* ads in the local paper for a week or two. Most of the ads probably won't mention a salary figure, but a few *may*. Among those that do, note what the lowest salary offering is, and what the highest is, and see if the ad reveals some reasons for the difference. It's interesting how much you can learn about salaries, with this approach. I know, because I was a secretary myself, once upon a time.

Another way to do salary research is to find a *Temporary Work Agency* that places secretaries, and let yourself be farmed out to various offices: the more, the merrier. It's relatively easy to do salary research when you're *inside* the place. (Study what that place pays *the agency*, not what the agency pays you.) If it's an office where the other workers *like* you, you'll be able to ask questions about a lot of things, including salary. It's like *summertime*, where the research is easy.

Before you finish your research, before you go in to that organization for your final interview, you want more than just one figure. You want *a range*. In any organization which has more than five employees, that range is relatively easy to figure out. It will be less than what the person *who would be above you* makes, and more than what the person *who would be below you* makes.

If The Person Who Would Be Below You Makes	And The Person Who Would Be Above You Makes	The Range For Your Job Would Be
$22,000	$27,000	$23,000 – $26,000
$10,000	$13,500	$10,500 – $12,500
$ 6,240	$ 7,800	$ 6,400 – $7,600

One teensy-tiny little problem: *how* do you find out the salary of those who would be above and below you? Well, first you have to find out their *names* or the names of their *positions*. If it is a small organization you are going after -- one with twenty or less employees -- finding this information out should be *duck soup*. Any employee who works there is likely to know the answer, and you can usually get in touch with one of those employees, or even an ex-employee, through your contacts. Since two-thirds of all new jobs are created by companies of that size, that's the size organization you are likely to be researching, anyway.

If you are going after a larger organization, then you have our familiar life-preserver to fall back on, namely, every contact you have (family, friend, relative, business, or church acquaintance) who might know the company, and therefore, the information you seek. You are looking for Someone Who Knows Someone who either is working, or has worked, at the particular place or places that interest you, who therefore has or can get this information for you.

If you absolutely run into a blank wall on a particular organization (everyone who works there is pledged to secrecy, and they have shipped all their ex-employees to Siberia), then seek out information on their nearest *competitor* in the same geographic area. *For example,* let us say you were researching Bank X, and they were proving to be inscrutable about what they pay their managers. You would then try Bank Y as your research base, to see if the information were easier to come by, there. And if it were, you would then assume the two were similar in their pay scales, and that what you learned about Bank Y was applicable also to Bank X.

Also experts say that in researching salaries, you should take note of the fact that most governmental agencies have civil service positions matching those in private industry, and their job descriptions and pay ranges are available to the public. Go to the nearest City, County, Regional, State, or Federal Civil Service office, find the job description nearest what you are seeking in private industry, and then ask for the starting salary.

When all this research is done, when you are in the actual hiring-interview, and the employer mentions the figure *they* have in mind, you are then ready to respond: "I understand of course the constraints under which all organizations are operating in the '90s, but I believe my productivity is such that it would *justify* a salary in the range of . . . " -- *and here you mention a figure near the top of* their *range.*

It will help a lot if during this discussion, you are prepared to show in what ways you will *make money* or in what ways you will *save money* for that organization, such as will justify the higher salary you are seeking. Hopefully, this will succeed in getting you the salary you want.[12]

During your salary negotiation, do not forget to pay attention to so-called fringe benefits. 'Fringes' such as life insurance, health benefits or health plans, vacation or holiday plans, and retirement programs typically add another 28% to many workers' salaries. That is to say, if an employee receives $800 salary per month, the fringe benefits are worth another $200 per month.

If your job is at a higher level, benefits may include but not be limited to: health, life, dental, disability, malpractice insurance; insurance for dependents; sick leave; vacation; personal leave/personal days; educational leave; educational cost reimbursement for coursework related to the job; maternity and or parental leave; health leave to care for dependents; bonus system or profit sharing; stock options; expense accounts for entertaining clients; dues to professional associations; travel reimbursement; fee sharing arrangements for clients that the employee generates; organizational memberships; parking; automobile allowance; relocation costs; sabbaticals; professional conference costs; time for community service; flextime work schedules; fitness center memberships.

You should therefore remember to ask what benefits are offered, and negotiate if necessary for the raises you want. Thinking this out ahead of time, of course, makes your negotiating easier, by far. You can prepare the ground during your salary negotiation, by saying: *"If I accomplish this job to your satisfaction, as I fully expect to -- and more -- when could I expect to be in line for a raise?"*

---

12. Daniel Porot, in Europe, suggests that if you and an employer really hit it off, and you're *dying* to work there, but they cannot afford the salary you need, consider offering them part of your time. If you need, and believe you deserve, say $25,000, but they can only afford $15,000, you might consider offering them three days a week of your time for that $15,000 (15/25 = 3/5). This leaves you free to take other work those other two days.

Once all salary negotiation is concluded to your satisfaction, do remember to ask to have it summed up in a letter of agreement -- or employment contract -- that they give to you. It may be you cannot get it in writing, but do try! The Road to Hell is paved with oral promises that went unwritten, and -- later -- unfulfilled.

Many executives unfortunately 'forget' what they told you during the hiring-interview, or even deny they ever said such a thing.

Also, many executives leave the company for another position and place, and their successor or the top boss may disown any *unwritten* promises: *"I don't know what caused them to say that to you, but they clearly exceeded their authority, and of course we can't be held to that."*

Plan to keep track of your accomplishments at this new job, on a weekly basis -- jotting them down, every weekend, in your own private diary. Career experts, such as Bernard Haldane, recommend you do this without fail. You can then summarize these accomplishments annually on a one-page sheet, for your boss's eyes, when raise or promotion is a legitimate subject for you to bring up.[13]

---

13. In any good-sized organization, you will often be amazed at how little attention your superiors pay to your noteworthy accomplishments, and how little they are aware at the end of the year that you really are *entitled* to a raise. Noteworthy your accomplishments may be, but no one is taking notes . . . unless *you* do.

What
To Do, When Employers Never Invite You Back

WHEN IT'S NOT YOUR FAULT

I hear regularly from job-hunters who report that they pay attention to all the matters I have mentioned in this chapter, and are quite successful at getting interviews -- but they still don't get hired. And they want to know what they're doing wrong. Well, unfortunately, the answer *sometimes* is: "Maybe nothing."

I don't know *how often* this happens, but I know it does happen -- because more than one employer has confessed it to me, and in fact at one point in my life it actually happened to *moi*: namely, *some* employers play games, whereby they invite you in for an interview despite the fact that they have already hired someone for the position in question!

You are cheered, of course, by the ease with which you get these interviews. But unbeknownst to you, the manager who is interviewing you (we'll say it's a *he*) has a personal friend he already agreed to give the job to. Of course, one small problem remains: the State or the Federal government gives funds to this organization, and has mandated that this position be opened to all. So this manager must comply. He therefore pretends to choose ten candidates, including his favorite, and pretends to interview them all as though the job opening were wide open and available. But, he intended, from the beginning, to reject the first nine and choose his favorite, and since you were selected for the honor of being among those nine, you automatically get rejected -- even if you are a much better candidate. This tenth person is, after all, his *friend.* The manager then claims that he followed the mandated hiring procedures to the letter.

If you are one of the nine, you will of course be baffled as to *why* you got turned down. Trouble is, you won't know if it was because you met an employer who was playing this game, or not. You're just depressed.

WHEN IT IS
YOUR FAULT

There is always the chance that no games are being played, by the employer: but you are getting rejected, at place after place, because there is something really wrong with the way you are coming across, during these hiring-interviews.

Employers will rarely ever tell you this. You will never hear them say something like, "You're too cocky and arrogant during the interview." You will almost always be left completely in the dark as to what it is you're doing wrong.

One way around this deadly silence, is to ask for *generalized* feedback, from whoever was the *friendliest* employer that you saw a while back. If your interviews, time and again, are leading nowhere, you can always try phoning them, reminding them of who you are, and then asking the following question -- deliberately kept generalized, vague, unrelated just to *that* place, and above all, *future-directed*: *"You know, I've been on several interviews at several different places now, where I've gotten turned down. From what you've seen, is there something about me in an interview, that is causing me not to get hired at those places? If so, I'd really appreciate your giving me some pointers so I can do better in my future hiring-interviews."*

Most of the time they'll *still* duck saying anything hurtful or helpful. First of all, they're afraid of lawsuits. Secondly, they don't know how you will use what they might have to say. (Said an old veteran to me once, "I used to think it was my duty to hit everyone with the truth. Now I only give it to those who can use it.")

But *occasionally* you will run into an employer who is willing to risk giving you the truth, because they think you know how to use it. In the absence of any such help from employers who interviewed you, you might want to get a good business friend of yours to role-play a mock hiring-interview with you, in case they see something glaringly wrong with how you're 'coming across.'

If, from either friend or employer-on-the-phone, you do get feedback, thank them from the bottom of your heart -- no matter how painful their feedback is. Such advice, seriously heeded, can bring about just the changes in your interviewing strategy that you most need, in order to win the interview.

When all else fails, I would recommend you go to a career counselor that charges by the hour, and put yourself in their tender knowledgeable hands.

Never
Put All Your Eggs In One Basket

In conclusion, I would like to say this: I have studied successful and unsuccessful job-hunters for over a quarter of a century, now, and the single greatest thing I have ever learned is that the secret of *successful* job-hunters is *that they always have alternatives*. Alternative ways of describing what they want to do. Alternative ways of going about the job-hunt (not just resumes, agencies, and ads). Alternative *job prospects*. Alternative 'target' organizations that they go after. Alternative ways of approaching employers. And so on, and so forth.

Be sure you have more than just one employer that you are pursuing. That organization, that office, that group, that church, that factory, that government agency, that volunteer organization may be *the ideal place* where you would like to work. But no matter how appetizing this *first choice* looks to you, no matter how much it makes your mouth water at the thought of working there, *you are committing job-hunting suicide* if you don't have some alternative places in mind. Sure, maybe you'll get that dream-come-true. But -- *big question* -- what are your plans if you don't? You've *got* to have other plans **now** -- not when that first target runs out of gas, three months from now. You must go after more than one organization. I recommend five, at least.

> ### Target Small Organizations
>
> Were I myself looking for a job tomorrow, this is what I would do. After I had figured out, as in the previous chapters, what my ideal job looked like, and after I had collected a list of those workplaces that have such jobs, in my chosen geographical area, I would then circle the names and addresses of those which are *small* organizations (personally I would restrict my *first draft* to those with 25 or less employees) -- and then go after them, in the manner I have described in this chapter. However, since small organizations can sometimes be static or dying, I would look particularly for small organizations that are **established** or **growing**. And if '*organizations with 25 or less employees*' eventually didn't turn up enough *leads* for me, only then would I broaden my search to '*organizations with 50 or less employees,*' and finally -- if that turned up nothing -- to '*organizations with 100 or less employees.*' But I would *start* small. Very small.

Remember, job-hunting always involves luck, to some degree. But with a little bit of luck, and a lot of hard work, plus determination, these instructions about how to get hired, should work for you, even as they have worked for so many hundreds of thousands before you.

Take heart from those who have gone before you, such as this determined job-hunter, who just wrote me this heartfelt letter, with which I close:

"Before I read this book, I was depressed and lost in the futile job-hunt using Want Ads Only. I did not receive even one phone call from any ad I answered, over a total of 4 months. I felt that I was the most useless person on earth. I am female, with a $2\frac{1}{2}$ year old daughter, former professor in China, with no working experience at all in the U.S. We came here seven months ago because my husband had a job offer here.

"Then, on June 11th of this year (1996), I saw your book in a local bookstore. Subsequently, I spent 3 weeks, 10 hours a day except Sunday, reading every single word of your book and doing all of the flower

petals in the Quick Job-Hunting Map. After getting to know myself much better, I felt I was ready to try the job-hunt again. I used Parachute throughout as my guide, from the very beginning to the very end, namely, salary negotiation.

"In just two weeks I secured (you guessed it) two job offers, one of which I am taking, as it is an excellent job, with very good pay. It is (you guessed it again) a small company, with 20 or so employees. It is also a career-change: I was a professor of English; now I am to be a controller!

"I am so glad I believed your advice: there are jobs out there, and there are two types of employers out there, and truly there are!

"I hope you will be happy to hear my story."

Other Resources

Additional materials by Richard N. Bolles to help you with your job-hunt:

JOB-HUNTING ON THE INTERNET
The inaugural book in our new Parachute Library, this stand-alone extract from *Parachute* is frequently updated with the latest and hottest Internet addresses and Websites for job-hunters of all types.

HOW TO CREATE A PICTURE OF YOUR IDEAL JOB OR NEXT CAREER
This 8½ by 11 inches workbook is designed to lead the reader through a series of detailed exercises, almost identical to The Workbook here in *Parachute*.

THE ANATOMY OF A JOB
This full size (24 by 36 inches) poster serves as a worksheet to supplement *How to Create a Picture of Your Ideal Job or Next Career* (described above). The "Skills Keys" are on one side, the "Flower" on the other.

HOW TO FIND YOUR MISSION IN LIFE
This is a gift-book version of the current Epilogue from *Parachute*. Judging by the mail the author receives, this is a favorite of readers who want their work to fulfill a purpose and bring more than simply money to their lives.

THE MISSION POSTER
This colorful 24-by-36-inch-poster summarizes the main ideas in *How to Find Your Mission in Life.*

JOB-HUNTING TIPS FOR THE SO-CALLED "HANDICAPPED" OR PEOPLE WHO HAVE DISABILITIES
Originally published as an appendix in *Parachute,* this popular resource is now available only as a separate booklet. In this work, Bolles uses his unique perspective on job-hunting and career-changes to address the special experiences of the disabled.

WHAT COLOR IS YOUR PARACHUTE? Audiotapes
Read by the author, this series of audiotapes supplements the book with additional material, including an introduction and overview of the job-hunting process, and a helpful question-and-answer session.

For more information, or to order, call the publisher at the number below. We accept VISA, Mastercard, and American Express. You may also wish to write for our free catalog of over 500 books, posters, and audiotapes.

Ten Speed Press • P.O. Box 7123 • Berkeley, CA 94707
800-841-BOOK

Update for 1998

TO: PARACHUTE
P.O. Box 379
Walnut Creek, CA 94597

I think that the information in the '97 edition needs to be changed, in your next revision, regarding (or, the following resource should be added):

_____

_____

_____

_____

_____

_____

I cannot find the following resource, listed on page _____:

_____

_____

_____

_____

_____

_____

Name _____

Address _____

Please make a copy.

Submit this so as to reach us by February 1, 1997. Thank you.